Beeswax
Crafting

Beeswax Crafting

Robert Berthold Jr.

with craft contributions by:

Margo Barraclough
Michael Bossom
Elizabeth A. Duffin

Edited by Lawrence J. Connor

Wicwas Press

Cheshire • Connecticut • 06410 • U.S.A.

Dedication

I dedicate this book to my wife Marren for her
encouragement, help and understanding.

Published 1993 by Wicwas Press
P. O. Box 817
Cheshire, Connecticut 06410-0817, USA

First Edition

Library of Congress Cataloging-in Publication Data:

Berthold, Robert.
    Beeswax crafting / Robert Berthold. Jr.: with craft contributions by
    Margo Barraclough, Michael Bossom, Elizabeth A. Duffin; edited by
    Lawrence J. Connor. —1st ed.
        128 p. cm.
    Includes bibliographical references and index.
    ISBN 1-878075-02-0
    1. Wax craft. 2. Beeswax. I. Connor, Lawrence John. II. Title.
TT866.B47 1993
        638'.17--dc20   93-19562
                                                                        CIP

ISBN Number: 1-878075-02-0

Table of Contents

List of Figures

Foreword

Beeswax is a truly unique and remarkable substance. In nature, beeswax serves as the foundation of the bee hive, providing efficient storage of honey and pollen, and a compact rearing area for immature bees. While some social wasps use chewed wood to form similar structures, the various species of honey bees are the only insects which have utilized wax to build the hexagon pattern so efficiently.

Beeswax was originally the only natural wax in use commercially. Even the word *wax*, which derived from the Old English *weax*, referred only to the wax of the honey bee kept in Europe. Since the early 19th century, the word wax has included other natural substances which resembled beeswax in some properties.

Beeswax is valuable, usually 2 to 3 times more valuable than vegetable waxes, and many times more valuable than waxes developed from petroleum.

For beekeepers, beeswax represents a valuable asset obtained from their bees. While beeswax was traditionally worth 5 times the value of honey, both products are now controlled by very different economic forces. Beeswax has a strong international market, and many developing countries depend upon the value of beeswax for export.

For many amateur beekeepers, beeswax is often over looked. Beekeepers can 'cash in' their wax for foundation wax for new honey combs. But they can also contact local hobby and craft shops and make wax available to local tradespeople. This way, the beekeeper can earn more for his or her wax than the current wholesale value, yet the craftsperson can buy top quality beeswax at a price far below the retail value. Craftspeople who use large amounts of beeswax are wise to call their extension agent or officer and find the names of local beekeepers. This could be an ideal arrangement for both parties!

This book started as an effort to publish Bob Berthold's notes and handouts. As we progressed, additional information was added and contributing authors were added to the project. I wish to give special thanks to Karl Showler of B & K Books, Hay-on-Wye, Wales, for critically reading an early draft. Since the craft field has many special terms and 'standard' procedures, Karl helped us see matters from an English viewpoint and made many useful suggestions.

Beeswax is used extensively in art and craft projects. There is a reason for this: beeswax posses unique characteristics which make it ideal for crafts like encaustic painting, batik and wax flower modeling. Sometimes used as 100% beeswax, and sometimes combined with other products to obtain special properties, beeswax permits these crafts to exist and flourish—I was surprised to find that beeswax (from Africanized bees) is in short supply in Trinidad because the batik artists deal directly with the beekeepers and buy up all the beeswax they can find.

Three craftspeople also joined the project. Liz Duffin and I had met at the National Honey Show in London, where her wax flower entry was the talk of the show. She and husband Mike have developed a wonderful set of slides, which have been extensively used in this book.

Michael Bossom was located through a friend of Liz Duffin. Michael is a commercial artist living in Glogue, Wales, where he specializes in encaustic painting. We appreciate the fact that he interrupted his very busy schedule to prepare materials for us.

Finally, we welcome Margo Barraclough as both artist, teacher and part of my wife's family. A school art teacher (now retired) Margo has taught batik to early teenagers in the Pittsburgh (Pennsylvania) public schools. Always popular in the art community, batik has become a very popular commercial medium. The artwork which I photographed for use in this section was created by Pamela Marshall, an artist living in Trinidad. I appreciate her permission to use her exciting designs.

Todd Yocher's efforts in proofreading, editing and serving as my assistant are greatly appreciated.

Beeswax Crafting incorporates the ideas from many sources and we appreciate the effort of any individual whose contribution is unrecognized in these pages.

Finally, we must recognize that some recipes and procedures may not work under all conditions. We ask readers to let us know about both their successes and failures when using this book.

Enjoy the book!

—Lawrence J. Connor, Editor and Publisher

Safety with Beeswax

Accidents with beeswax can be deadly. Never heat beeswax with an open flame. While beeswax is difficult to ignite as a solid, liquid beeswax will spread and burn rapidly. Even small amounts of water, when improperly mixed with beeswax, will lead to a potential explosion or boiling over of beeswax. Extreme caution should be used when working with wax.

Prior planning is a big help in cleanup. Flattened paper boxes will serve as a good floor and table covering and can be reused or discarded after a wax project is completed. On tile or smooth concrete floors, spilled wax may be scraped off and the residual wax removed by buffing. Wax spilled on carpets is nearly impossible to remove; the cost of cleaning may exceed the cost of replacement!

Prepare your work area carefully, choose your materials with concern for cleanup and use extreme caution while working with wax. Keep small children and pets out of the work area. A few minutes of planning will often reduce countless headaches later.

A few hints to eliminate problems:

- Use electricity for your heat source—no flame
- Heat wax in a water bath
- Use a container with a safe handle
- Don't overheat beeswax - it discolors at 85°C (185°F)
- Empty your wax pot after each use—avoid explosions!
- Never melt wax from below only—melt from the sides
- When dipping, allow for displacement or wax will overflow
- Use a container with a handle and pouring lip
- If wax spills on the skin, run under cold water and peel off
- No small children, no unsupervised children, no pets

Introduction

I started beekeeping with used equipment which included numerous old, black combs. I removed each comb from its frame and replaced them with new beeswax foundation. I then attempted to "render" the combs into beeswax. Unfortunately, it resembled road tar.

With my prized possession in hand, I decided to make beeswax candles. In my complete bliss, never having seen a beeswax candle, never having made any type of candle, and never having read about candlemaking, I started out to make a beeswax candle. I used a metal orange juice can with the top cut out and a small hole punched in the other end as my mold. I found a piece of string (not candle wick) in my mother's kitchen drawer and was all set to make candles. It was trial-and-error until I found a method to keep the wax from escaping from the can. When the molding process was finally completed, the candle would not release from the mold. After many tries, I finally cut the can using a hacksaw. With Thanksgiving approaching, I proudly presented my pitch-black work-of-art to mother. Like most parents, she was very pleased with the gift made by her son, and she proudly displayed the candle on our dining room table. When Thanksgiving Day arrived and with family and friends present, the candle was lit with great fanfare.

It was a Thanksgiving dinner that has gone down in the annals of our family history. The "beeswax candle", once lit, began to sputter, to spark, and to produce a lot of smoke. It is surprising what a Roman candle effect a beeswax candle loaded with propolis and pupal cases can have! Fortunately the candle soon extinguished itself with accompanying comments of "my son the beekeeper" and "my son the candlemaker". After a few days, the candle "mysteriously" disappeared from the table, and although I knew that my mother was holding her breath wondering if I would notice she had removed it, I expelled a big sigh of relief that the abomination was gone.

Years later, while a graduate student at Pennsylvania State Univrsity, beekeeping extension specialist Bill Clarke suggested that I make beeswax candles for Christmas gifts. He said that he did this yearly, and they were so appreciated by those that he gave them to. I thought back to my initial candlemaking experience, but instead of rejecting his idea outright, I asked him how he made beeswax candles. He said that he used an antique mold, clean beeswax and candle wicking. My wife quickly obtained an antique mold, and although it presented problems with leaks, dents and rust-finished early candles, I was into the candlemaking business. We did give candles as gifts that first year, as we have done ever since, and they were and are much appreciated. My mother was a bit hesitant about her first set, but she did give them a try and found them to be a great improvement over my first attempt!

After being awarded my Doctorate by Pennsylvania State University, I settled in at Delaware Valley College, in Doylestown, PA, and became their beekeeping specialist, along with many other duties. For 10 summers I worked as a regional apiary inspector for the Pennsylvania Department of Agriculture. During my travels as an inspector, I continually encountered beekeepers who had accumulated a lifetime's supply of beeswax. Most of them were aware that they could sell the wax, but most did not want to make the effort. I even encountered some who were throwing their wax away rather than to be "bothered" with it. This stimulated me to compile a list of uses for beeswax. As time passed, I started to incorporate this information into the beekeeping courses that I teach, into workshops that various beekeeping groups began to ask me to do, and into articles published in the various beekeeping magazines.

This book, then, is a compilation of many uses of beeswax. Many people over the years have supplied me with information which is included in this publication. We have found that due to variations in beeswax and additives, you should experiment on a small scale before deciding to go into commercial production.

—*Robert Berthold Jr.*
Doylestown, Pennsylvania

Chapter I

Figure I.1. Bees festoon in open spaces where comb is to be built and secrete beeswax.

What is Beeswax?

How bees make wax

Beeswax is produced by four pairs of glands located on the underside of the worker bee's abdomen (Figure I.2). The bees which produce the wax rest quietly while their bodies convert honey into beeswax. They use the sugar in honey to make the wax, and nothing else. If you confine bees to a closed container, and feed them only pollen (the other food of the bees), they produce no beeswax. When bees are fed a diet of just sugar syrup, they produce beeswax. The bee's digestive system digests the sugars in honey, and, in the right age bee, this stimulates the wax glands to secrete wax. The wax glands cover areas called mirrors; the wax is secreted as a liquid through the porous mirrors and it hardens into small flakes in wax pockets between the mirrors and the preceding

Figure I.2. Beeswax is produced by four pairs of glands located on the underside of the worker bee's abdomen.

Figure I.3. The bee transfers the wax scale to her mouth where she manipulates it with her mandibles, mixing and kneading it with salivary secretions.

Figure I.4. The worker bee uses her jaw-like mandibles to carry the softened wax to parts of the hive where fresh wax is being built into comb.

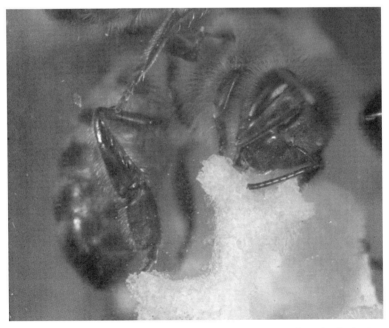

Figure I.5. The bee adds the softened wax to existing pieces of comb which IS in construction within the beehive.

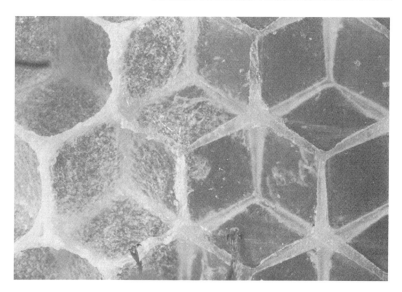

Figure I.6. Beekeepers give their bees sheets of beeswax which have had the hexagon pattern milled onto the surface. Bees add wax to this foundation.

segment. The worker bee then uses the last row of bristles on the first tarsal joints of her hind legs to hook the wax flake out of its abdominal pocket. She then transfers the wax flake to her mouth where she chews it with her mandibles, mixing and kneading it with salivary secretions (Figures I.3, I.4 and I.5). These beeswax plates are almost pure white when first produced, but they take on a lemony-yellow color due to the addition of propolis and other natural products of the beehive, such as honey, pollen and the pigments from pupal skins in brood comb (Figure I.7).

Comb construction

Wax production and shaping require a minimum temperature of 90°F (32°C). Comb construction starts at or near the top of the nest. Bees build their combs vertically downward from a horizontal or a nearly horizontal surface. They build the comb out to 1/8" (3.2 mm) or more in thickness at the place of attachment for strength. The combs are usually one-inch thick (25.4 mm) with 3/8" to 1/2" (9.5 mm to 12.7 mm) bee space[1] between them. There is considerable variation in the thickness of combs: brood combs are uniform in thickness while honey

[1] The bee space is the distance between surfaces in which bees will not build comb or fill with propolis.

combs may be considerably thicker. The cells of the comb are built with an inclination of about 13° upward. The combs are two-sided and share a common base. This, coupled with the hexagon shape of the cells, provides the optimum utilization of materials versus strength. Engineers use the "honeycomb design" when they require lightweight construction and optimum strength.

The average age of a worker bee involved in comb construction is 16 days. The work of the wax workers seems quite inefficient. One bee attaches a bit of wax, while another bee removes it and attaches it somewhere else (Figures I.4 and I.5). Additional wax is added and the comb grows. The wax deposition-removal-redeposition may produce a more durable material. Bees apparently add salivary secretions to the wax during this reworking process.

Figure I.7. Wax takes on a lemony-yellow color due to the addition of pollen and other sources such as honey, propolis and pigments from pupal skins in brood comb.

The attachment of the comb at the top of the nest is more intensive while the bottom and the lower corners hang free. To add additional strength and to provide walkways, the bees add brace and bridge combs. The bees also use their wax to seal over cells of ripe honey; these are the wax cappings of the honey comb. If the bees leave an airspace between the honey and the wax, the capping will appear light in color. If the bees do not leave such an airspace, the capping will appear dark or "watery". Comb honey customers prefer their honey this way because of the magnificent taste treat. The wax is inert and safe to eat.

Physical and chemical properties of beeswax

Beeswax is classified as an organic compound made up primarily of carbon, hydrogen and oxygen atoms. Chemical analysis reveals that there are over 300 individual components in beeswax, most of them in trace amounts and some which may be contaminants. While beeswax varies from sample to sample, Bisson, Vansell and Dye (1940) found that virgin beeswax, as collected directly from the wax glands of honey bees, is very consistent chemically and physically, and that most changes resulted from the beeswax's contact with other materials in the hive and during its processing.

Chemical profile

The average chemical profile for a large number of beeswax samples from European honey bees (*Apis mellifera*) was found by Tulloch (1980) to contain the following:

35% monoesters
14% diesters
14% hydrocarbons
12% free acids
8% hydroxy polyesters
4% hydroxy monoesters
3% triesters
2% acid polyesters
1% acid esters
1% free alcohols
6% unidentified

The esters, alcohols and fatty acids are made up of long-chain hydrocarbons which contribute to three major characteristics of beeswax. Hydrocarbons are not digestible by most organisms, they are chemically inert and insoluble in water and they are solid at hive temperatures providing mechanical stability.

Bees which produce beeswax

The "western" honey bee (*Apis mellifera*) evolved in Europe, western Asia and Africa. It was introduced into North and South America, Australia, Asia and other areas. Other honey bees are found in Asia, ranging from the tiny *Apis florea* to the giant *Apis dorsata*. *Apis cerana* is the "eastern" honey bee, and is very similar to the western *mellifera*. Each species of honey bee produces a slightly different type of beeswax, containing different components and chemical ratios. These

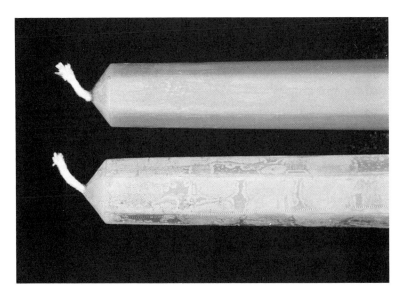

Figure I.8. Beeswax which has been stored in a cool place can develop a dusty appearance called bloom, shown on the bottom candle.

properties can be used to identify the source of a sample of beeswax. Beeswax standards used in North America, Africa, Australia and other countries are based upon the western honey bee. Readers should consult Tulloch (1980) for further information. Other bees, like bumble-bees, also produce wax, but because of its extreme rareness it is not discussed here.

Beeswax as compared to other natural waxes

Many waxes are found in nature. Waxes are collected from plant sources, such as palm, bayberry, and other species. These waxes are found in the surface of the leaves, and are part of the plant's natural protection from the outside environment. Plant waxes are relatively hard, crystalline in nature, and have high melting points.

Beeswax has a 10 to 20°C lower melting point than plant waxes. Tulloch (1980) states that this lower melting point is due to the large number of different chemicals found in beeswax, as well as the physical properties of these molecules. This lower melting point permits the bees a softened wax for working in the brood nest for comb construction. This property is used by the craftspeople to their advantage. It permits one to mold and shape beeswax by hand, or to use lower heat in the processing of the wax.

Figure I.9. Since beeswax is very brittle at low temperature, and solid at room temperature, it may be cut much like one would cut wood. However, it is sometimes easier to melt beeswax rather than to cut it.

Physical profile

Beeswax melts at 147.9±1.0°F (64.4±0.6°C); its solidity point (the point where liquid wax becomes solid) is 146.3±1.0°F (63.5±0.5°C); its density at 68°F (20°C) is 0.963, which means that it is less dense than water (density of water = 1.0) and therefore beeswax floats; and its refractive index (light bending property) at 176°F (80°C) is 1.4402. Beeswax's flash point is 490-525°F (254-274°C) depending upon the purity of the wax. A free-standing block of beeswax will melt away from a flame rather than ignite (Coggshall and Morse 1984). For this reason, always use an electric element to heat beeswax rather than using an open flame. Extreme caution should always be used when heating beeswax.

For comparison, ordinary paraffin melts between 90°-150°F (32°-66°C) and microcrystalline paraffin melts between 150°-185°F (66°-85°C), depending upon the length of the hydrocarbon chain.

Beeswax is very brittle at room temperature and large blocks of wax must be cut much like a piece of wood (Figure I.9). Beeswax foundation, candles, etc. must be handled very carefully at cold temperatures to avoid cracking and breaking. Above 90°F (32°C), beeswax is very malleable and is ideal for carving and hand forming. After being heated to about 200°F (93.3°C), beeswax shrinks approximately 10% when

Figure I.10. When beeswax candles are burned, they produce white, round flames. These candles smoke the least of all types of candles.

cooled to room temperature (77°F; 25°C). This is important when making candles in molds, since heating the wax to 180°F (82.2°C) causes the candle to contract from the sides of the mold as it cools. This facilitates candle removal but also necessitates the re-topping of the candle as it cools.

Beeswax is a stable compound as evidenced by encaustic paintings dating back thousands of years and beeswax samples found in the pyramids and Roman ruins.

Bloom

Beeswax which has been stored in a cool place can develop a dusty appearance called bloom (Figure I.8). The exact cause of bloom is still unclear but seems to be linked to a chemical change in the structure of the wax molecules on the surface[2]. Bloom does not ruin the wax and is a natural phenomena. For the craftsperson, this patina can be a concern, since it will change the appearance of the final product containing beeswax, especially in candles and carved wax.

---

[2] Microscopic examination of bloom reveals that it is made up of flat, transparent, refractive plates without uniform symmetry. Its melting point is 104°F (39°C) and its solidifying point is 102°C (37.5°F). It is soluble in hydrochloric acid or sodium hydroxide after 14 hours; insoluble in 95% ethyl alcohol or water; very soluble in carbon tetrachloride, benzene and carbon disulfide. When burned it leaves no ash. I believe that it might be produced by molecular rearrangements occurring under optimum temperature conditions causing changes in the volume of the wax with the extrusion of some of its low-melting plastic components.

Figure I.11. When beeswax candles are burned next to paraffin candles, the beeswax candles usually burn more slowly. This is influenced by the wax mixture (in paraffin candles), the level of impurities in both, and the wick size and shape.

Some people like bloom on their beeswax candles while others don't care for it. Some rub candles with a piece of cloth to remove it. This works quite well for tapers and other smooth candles, but it can be quite tedious for items with intricate designs. To eliminate bloom, we set wax items in a warm greenhouse[3] until the bloom disappears. We have also used a hair dryer or warm water to remove the bloom. This warming of the surface of the wax appears to reverse the changes which created the bloom in the first place.

Burning beeswax

When beeswax candles are burned, they produce white, round flames (Figure I.10). These candles smoke the least of all types of candles depending upon the purity of the wax and the wicking used when the candle was made. The purity of the wax also influences the aroma that the burning of the candles produces. Since beeswax has a greater viscosity when melted than most other types of wax, beeswax candles tend to burn longer than commercially made paraffin candles. Based on our research, we found that beeswax candles burn up to twice as long as non-beeswax candles of the same size (Figure I.11). This helps the customer justify the expense of beeswax candles.

[3] One day after returning from a beeswax workshop, I noticed that some candles that originally were covered with bloom had regained their glossy finish after spending a number of hours in the sun-heated trunk of my car. After a couple of simple experiments, we found that heat will remove the bloom. We have found the 100+°F (38+°C) temperatures in our greenhouse will remove the bloom from our beeswax candles.

Chapter II

Figure II.1. Beekeepers remove cappings in order to harvest honey. These cappings produce excellent wax for craft use.

Processing Beeswax

Beeswax sources

Beekeepers obtain beeswax from three sources within the hive: cappings[4] (Figure II.1), combs and hive scrapings. If the beekeeper is planning to use wax for candlemaking, he or she should use only the wax obtained from cappings or which was rendered from comb in which no brood rearing occurred. These two sources will provide a clean

---

[4] Cappings are obtained from filled and sealed combs of honey. The beekeeper uses a heated knife to cut and remove the top of the honey comb in order to spin the honey out of the comb in a device called a honey extractor. The wax cappings contain honey, and are delicious to eat because the wax is very thin and extremely delicate. This wax and honey mixture is separated and the wax becomes capping wax.

burning wax with a lemony-yellow color. Certain plants produce wax with distinctive color and/or aroma based upon the nectar their flowers secrete. Wax obtained by rendering old comb or scrapings, although dark in color, may be used in non-candlemaking endeavors, and if properly cleaned, it can be used for making colored candles.

Beeswax rendering

CAUTION: MELTED WAX IS HIGHLY FLAMMABLE. MANY BEEKEEPERS HAVE STARTED SERIOUS FIRES THROUGH THE IMPROPER MELTING OF BEESWAX. NEVER EXPOSE BEESWAX TO AN OPEN FLAME. COVER YOUR WORK AREA, INCLUDING THE FLOOR, WITH SOME TYPE OF WATERPROOF (WAX PROOF) DROP CLOTH OR COATED BOARD.

Risk of wax contamination

Prior to rendering, the beeswax should be as free from natural materials such as honey, propolis, pollen, etc., and contaminants as possible. While beeswax is remarkably stable under a wide range of conditions, it is easy to contaminate under special circumstances. This is due to its delicate nature, great stickiness and complex chemical composition. Capping wax should be drained, spun in a metal basket in a honey extractor, rinsed with cool water to remove any remaining honey and carefully air dried. The cappings should be placed in containers for dry storage, or rendered as quickly as possible. Moist cappings can support fermentation and/or mold growth, which will contaminate the wax. In particular, the natural odor of wax may be lost from the wax. Fermentation can develop quickly under certain conditions, so the only solution is to store the cappings dry until your are able to render them.

The use of certain metals during processing will cause discoloration of the wax. Avoid iron, brass, zinc and copper. Iron is especially harmful to wax, and will cause considerable darkening. There is little or no discoloration when beeswax is processed in stainless steel, aluminum, nickel, glass, Pyrex™ or tin.

Heat is a hazard to beeswax, causing darkening. Avoid direct heat from an electric coil or heating unit when beeswax is rendered. Not only will this darken the wax, but it will heat propolis and produce an offesnsive odor in the wax. This is especially a problem with dark wax.

Unprocessed cappings, combs and scrapings are highly attractive to wax moths, which produce larvae (much like corn borers) which feed on the materials found in beeswax. Wax moths will destroy combs very rapidly in hot and humid conditions, and are a particular problem in the warm weather of late summer and early fall. The larvae will destroy brood combs and highly stained honey supers. Once beeswax is rendered and kept in clean blocks, wax moths are much less of a problem unless the blocks contain pollen, cocoons and other materials.

Solar wax extractor

There are a number of different ways of rendering beeswax, some of which involve expensive equipment. An efficient and relatively inexpensive way of rendering beeswax is a solar wax extractor. Pennsylvania State University Professor Anderson found that solar wax extractors should be relatively airtight, covered with two panes of glass separated by about a 1/2" space, painted black on the outside and white on the inside and should have a tray in the bottom of the extractor to carry the molten wax into a collecting pan (Figure II.2) made of a material that can stand the high heat generated in the extractor. Iron, galvanized metals and copper should be avoided since they tend to darken the wax. A Teflon™-lined bread pan with sloped sides works well as a collecting pan. Hardened in the pan, and cooled overnight to

Figure II.2. The solar wax extractor is ideal for rendering small quantities of cappings, honey combs, and hive scrapings. It is not highly efficient for removing wax from dark brood combs. The secret is to process small amounts of wax every warm sunny day. Consult Appendix A for construction instructions.

get full shrinkage, the wax can be removed. A piece of screening placed between the wax and the collecting tray can be used to filter out larger contaminants such as pupal cases in old combs. To help the filtering process, cover the collecting pan with fine mesh nylon cloth or nylon stocking. Plans and instructions for building your own solar wax extractor are located in Appendix A.

Optimal output from a solar extract occurs when the inside temperature reaches 54°C (130°F) above the outside temperature. This requires very warm conditions; double layers of glass and a well-insulated black-colored box are essential for proper operation. Any honey which is obtained from the solar extractor should be buried since it has been overheated and may be caramelized.

Wax press and steam chest

Larger beekeepers may wish to use a wax press and/or steam chest for more efficient removal of wax. The dark material in a brood comb is called slumgum, and contains considerable wax. The use of a press releases this wax. Thin layers of combs placed in clean coarse woven sacks of burlap (jute or hemp) are layered in hot water, or preferably in

Figure II.3. A wax press is the most practical method of recovering beeswax from combs and slumgum. Various press systems exist. This is the simplest system—using bags of wax in a hot water bath to draw off the beeswax. since beeswax is lighter than water, the beeswax will float to the top of the water, where it may be drawn off or allowed to cool as a solid layer. Water pH may interfere—high alkali water will cause problems with this system. See page 30 for additional information.

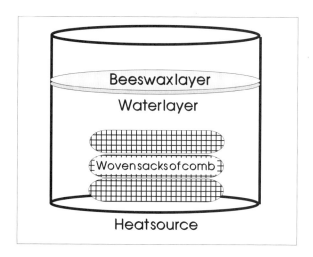

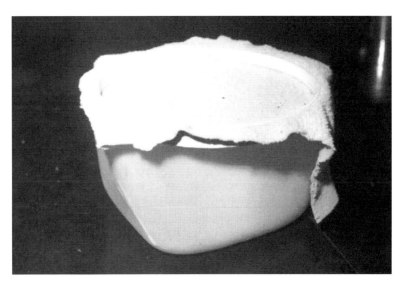

Figure II.4. A simple beeswax filter may be constructed from an embroidery hoop holding an absorbent material like old sweat-suit fabric. Filter all the wax at one time; once the wax hardens the fabric must be replaced.

a steam chest. The use of a press arrangement will extract additional wax. As the wax melts, it is filtered as it escapes through the coarse woven sack. In a commercial steam chamber, a gate allows the wax to be drawn from the chamber.

A simple water bath may be used where the bag of comb is weighted at the bottom of the tank containing heated water (Figure II.3). The wax can then be ladled off the surface of the water and poured into Teflon™-lined bread pans or other containers. This may cause the formation of wax emulsions where water is incorporated into the wax, and the emulsion is difficult to break. Certain water types favor this process; the use of distilled water may reduce the risk of emulsion formation, or so will adding a small amount of vinegar (weak acetic acid) to the water.

Once the wax has solidified, the blocks can then be turned over and any contaminants found on their underside can be scraped off. If the wax is still not clean enough, filter it through sweat-suit fabric with the smooth side of the cloth down. I often support filter cloth in an embroidery hoop (Figure II.4).

For small-scale batches of wax, a single thickness of paper towel can also be supported over a piece of window screen for filtering. The wax must be at least 180°F (80°C) or it will not pass through the paper filter. With either filtering method, once you stop pouring the liquid wax

Mixing wax and water—A warning!

When we presented this book to Karl Showler (Hay-on-Wye, Wales) for comment, he was adamantly opposed to the use of water in any wax melting technique, saying: "Much of the United Kingdom sits on chalk, and the water is very alkaline. If you boil beeswax and water together, you will get a spongy, worthless mess. We can never recommend the boiling of wax and water together in the U.K. or the readers will think the book is all wrong."

The water in eastern Pennsylvania, where the author resides, is undoubtedly acidic (hard). So it has been rare for the author to experience any difficulty when heating beeswax in water. As Bob Berthold explains:

"My system is homemade and uses heated water in direct contact with the wax. A heating element heats the water, into which I place the wax for melting. While I have used this system for over 25 years, there are two problems you may experience. First never let the wax cool in the processor with the water underneath. If you heat the water, it will expand, and may cause an explosion! Second, some areas have water which will cause the wax and water to mix, to emulsify, a process called saponification. The resulting wax-water mixture is difficult to reclaim. So, if you are still interested in my homemade processor, you may find instructions in Appendix B for its construction."

I suggest you experiment with a small batch of water and wax before you attempt a large batch. Let the wax and water cool overnight, and check for any softness or sponginess in the resulting wax. Natural beeswax is quite hard at room tempera ture.

You may try adding vinegar to the water (vinegar is a weak acid) and will neutralize alkaline water. But make a test batch first.

Water pH varies in many parts of the world. The wax in Figure II.5 was processed from old combs in Texas, and clearly shows softness and sponginess, indicating high alkaline water.

A final note: most commercial beekeepers use a capping melter to separate wax from honey. These melters usually produce an excellent quality wax, and I suggest craftspeople use capping melter wax whenever they can. So the water is not necessary.   —Editor

Figure II.5. Spongy wax after melting wax and alkali water together.

through the filter and the wax hardens, it is very difficult to get additional liquid wax to pass through it.

A wax processing tank

I use a wax processing tank to remove impurities from the wax produced in the solar extractor, or from one of the other methods used to produce blocks of beeswax. A wax processing tank may also be used by the craftsperson who desires an efficient method of producing large numbers of candles or wax products. The ideal tank has a water jacket, so that the wax is heated by hot water, and not with a heating element. Several beekeeping supply firms manufacture water-jacketed tanks which are suitable for melting beeswax and serve as a dipping tank for candles (Figure II.6). Wax should always be removed from the tank and cooled in smaller containers whenever you finish a project. Fortunately, the tank may be left on, at a lower setting, keeping the wax liquid while you take short breaks. The wax should be drained whenever you stop work for a long period of time, since wax will darken with prolonged heating.

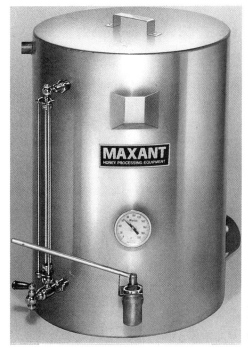

Figure II.6. A commercially made wax processing and dipping tank. This uses a water jacket to heat the wax and is very safe to use.

Beeswax bleaching and filtering

Sometimes beekeepers want to lighten the color of their beeswax. Newly produced beeswax flakes are almost pure white. If the beeswax flakes are collected as soon as they are produced by the four pairs of abdominal wax glands of the worker bees, it is almost pure white. In nature, the wax takes on color from contact with pollen, honey, propolis and pupal debris left in the brood cells. The beekeeper can darken wax by melting it in containers made from iron, copper, brass, Monel™ (iron-nickel-copper alloy) and zinc (galvanized metal). The ions of these metals cause wax to darken.

Most people expect beeswax candles to be a lemony color but it is not always so. One year I disqualified a wax entry that was very pale in color and did not have a typical beeswax aroma. I thought that the beekeeper had rendered commercial beeswax foundation. The wax entrant informed me that his wax entry had been produced by explicitly following the instructions I had given him! I have since learned that certain honey sources will produce very pale beeswax.

Commercially prepared beeswax is not bleached, but filtered. Firms use of a series of filtrations to remove the color of the wax, so the final product is white. Bleached wax is not acceptable to many commercial users, since bleaching changes the chemical nature of the wax. For

Figure II.7. The author's wax processing tank, which uses a water layer to heat the wax. Directions for home manufacture are shown in Appendix B. Please read the editor's warning on page 30 regarding the hazards of mixing water and wax. This tank must always be drained at the end of every use to prevent the risk of explosion when the wax is reheated!

Figure II.8. A commercial wax processing operation in Chiang Mai, Thailand. Notice the open flame beneath. If iron kettles were used, they were discoloring the wax. In this operation, old combs were heated in the kettles, and the liquid wax was transferred to enamel pans for cooling (see II.10). This operation had tons of beeswax in storage (see Figure II.9).

beekeepers who require white wax, we suggest that they sell their beeswax to larger firms and buy their filtered wax. Large wax handlers should investigate the use of a wax filtering system rather than bleaching.

The idea of bleaching beeswax goes back to the Greeks. They first flaked their beeswax and bleached it in the sun, boiled it in sea water, skimmed off the scum layer floating on top and repeated the boiling process. They then reflaked the wax and once again sun-bleached it. In the early 1900s, commercial beeswax processors were still using large greenhouses to utilize sunlight to bleach beeswax, much like the early Greeks did.

Dr. Jonathan White, the retired United States Department of Agriculture (USDA) specialist on honey and beeswax, developed a method to restore the light lemony color to beeswax that had been "abused" by the beekeeper through processing in the wrong type of container. He used 1/4 oz. of the sodium salt of ethylenediamine tetracetic acid per gallon of soft water (1.88 grams/liter of water)[5]. This

---

[5] If you have hard water in your area, it is suggested to add about 1/4 cup per gallon of vinegar to the water, otherwise the hardness of the water will cause some of your wax to emulsify with the water. See warning on page 30.

compound is a chelating agent, a material which binds with metal ions that cause beeswax to discolor. One gallon of the solution is needed for each 3.5 lbs. of wax. The wax is melted in the solution using a container made of stainless steel or glass (not enamel) and is held at 210°F for one hour during which time the mixture is continually stirred. The container is then removed from the heat and allowed to slowly cool. The block of wax is then removed and the residue on the bottom of the block is scraped off. The clean block is then re-melted in clean water, stirred briefly, and again allowed to cool. Any additional residue on the bottom of the block should be scraped off.

One effective bleaching agent is oxalic acid. Unfortunately, oxalic acid is a deadly poison and its use is not recommended. The material is either illegal to use or difficult to obtain in most countries. Permits are required in many countries to purchase oxalic acid.

Of other potential oxidizing agents, 30% hydrogen peroxide worked the best, although sodium dichromate, sodium permanganate, potassium permanganate, ammonium persulfate and benzoyl peroxide also work. Extreme caution must be used when handling any chemical.

Reagent grade (30% to 50%) hydrogen peroxide can also be used as a bleaching agent. It used to be available in most beauty salons because it was used as a bleaching agent for hair. With the advent of

Figure II.9. A commercial beekeeper's wax inventory. Wax may be stored like this for years, in 'rough' form. Color variations are due to different floral sources the bees visited while gathering nectar and from different age combs.

modern hair products, it is not as easily obtainable locally but is available commercially. The hydrogen peroxide reacts with the metal ions which cause the wax to darken. During the reaction, the hydrogen peroxide breaks down releasing oxygen and the metal ions precipitate out. Various methods have been used in bleaching beeswax with hydrogen peroxide and you should experiment to determine the amount of water and hydrogen peroxide to use per weight of wax before going into large-scale processing. No matter what method you use, you should do your melting in a stainless steel, Pyrex™ or enamel container, which should never be more than 3/4 full to prevent your mixture from boiling over. One method involves melting wax in water, maintaining the wax at that temperature, and then adding hydrogen peroxide. Stirring the wax-water-peroxide mixture will help expedite the bleaching process. In a second method, you can boil beeswax for 30 to 45 minutes in water containing 1% hydrogen peroxide.

CAUTIONS. If you need to obtain small quantities of white wax, consider trading your wax for filtered wax from a large wax processor. If not, remember the following:

1. *Wear protective clothing including gloves, long sleeve shirt, pants and glasses.*
2. *Never breath the vapors. Work in a place with good ventilation.*
3. *Avoid getting chemicals on yourself. If this should happen, follow the instructions on the label and seek medical attention if necessary.*
4. *If chemicals get on your clothing, remove clothing and launder.*
5. *Clean up all spills.*
6. *Properly store reagent in labeled containers in a secure place out of reach of children, pets, etc.*
7. *Properly dispose of used reagents.*

Figure II.10. Enamel pans filled with beeswax which has been extracted from cappings (light wax) or brood combs (dark wax).

Chapter III

Figure III.1. Most common cosmetics contain a portion of beeswax as an essential part of the formula.

Beeswax in Cosmetics and Pharmaceuticals

Beeswax does not cause allergic reactions in humans when applied to the skin. It is inert and may be safely ingested as a coating on pills to delay release of the contents. Beeswax is neither digested or absorbed by the body. Beeswax eaten with honey has no effect on the human system.

Due to its hypo-allergenic quality, beeswax is used extensively in the manufacture of cosmetics. The manufacture of cosmetics is the biggest use of beeswax, utilizing between 35-45% of all imported beeswax (International Trade Centre 1978). Some of the cosmetic uses

Beeswax usage, as a percentage of world beeswax use.
cosmetics   35-45
pharmaceutical preparations   25-30
candles   20
minor uses   10-20
(from Crane 1990)

of beeswax include the manufacture of lotions, facial creams, skin softeners, hand creams, ointments, lipstick, eye shadow, rouge, salves and epilators (hair remover). It is even used in camouflage face creams for military troops.

The use of beeswax in cosmetics and pharmaceuticals dates back to at least the Greek physician Galen (AD 130-201). He mixed beeswax, olive oil and water to make a cold cream for skin cleansing. The product was not stable, since the olive oil turned rancid. Until 1890, local pharmacies (chemists) would make small amounts of beeswax-based cold cream for customers (Coggshall and Morse 1984). Beeswax holds water in ointments (up to 50%) and stiffens the resulting product. It mixes with a wide range of organic compounds and is used in many emulsified and dispersed pharmaceutical products for skin applications (Crane 1990).

In products which must spread water over the skin, such as creams and lotions, the wax is usually emulsified by reaction with an alkali compound like borax. The borax saponifies the acids in beeswax to form a product which is technically a soap. Only 6.8 parts of borax are needed to neutralize the fatty acids in 100 parts of beeswax. If too much borax is used, the resulting cream will have a rough texture (Crane 1990).

Lipstick contains between 20-25% beeswax due its relatively high melting point and its ability to produce a good consistency and a high sheen. On average, eye shadow contains 6% beeswax, mascara 12%, hair creams 8% and epilators 20% (Crane 1990).

Commercial epilator products contain a mixture of oil, resin and wax with a melting temperature which is lower than any of the individual components. This permits the application of the epilator at a melting point without danger of burning. The paste-like material is melted and applied in a very thin coat to the part of the body where hair removal is desired. The treated area is then covered with a thin strip of muslin cloth pressed firmly to the skin. The skin is then pulled taut and the muslin strip is pulled off in the opposite direction of the hair growth.

There are alternate materials to beeswax available to cosmetic manufacturers, such as paraffin wax. However only 1% to 3% beeswax will give the final product the desirable effect, and it is very hard for a cosmetics manufacturer to avoid the use of beeswax (Coggshall and Morse 1984).

Below are some recipes for the home manufacture of beeswax containing cosmetics. In all cases, the recipes can be modified to meet your requirements. All melting of ingredients should be done in a stainless steel or heat-resistant glass double boiler (a container in a water bath), and the finished products placed in jars with tight-fitting lids. Use a stainless steel spoon or glass rod to stir the ingredients.

Beeswax-Almond Hand Cream

Ingredients

1 part beeswax
2 parts coconut oil
2 parts almond oil
1 part rose water

Directions

Heat oils and rose water, adding beeswax when the mixture reaches 150°F. Blend completely and package.

Yellow Ointment

Ingredients

50 grams beeswax
950 grams petrolatum

Directions

Heat petrolatum, adding beeswax when the mixture reaches 150°F. Blend completely and package.

Cold Cream

Ingredients

62% colorless mineral oil
10% beeswax
28% distilled water
Trace of borax

Directions

Blend all ingredients in a double boiler, blending with a stainless steel spoon.

Skin Softener

Ingredients

4 tablespoons strained freshly squeezed lemon
        juice
2 tablespoons liquid lecithin
2 tablespoons olive oil
1 tablespoon flaked beeswax

Directions

Blend all ingredients by heating in a double boiler, blending with a stainless steel spoon. Store in a screw top jar in the refrigerator.

Hand Cream with Bee Pollen

Ingredients

2 parts beeswax
3 parts glycerin
3 parts petroleum jelly
2 tablespoons of bee pollen

Directions

Melt beeswax with glycerin and petroleum jelly then blend in pollen. (While allergies to beeswax are unknown, allergies to pollen are reported. Always try bee pollen on a small area of the skin to test for reaction).

Hand Cream with Coconut Oil

Ingredients

3 parts beeswax
3 parts coconut oil
4 parts glycerin
3 tablespoons of baby oil

Directions

Melt all ingredients together and blend.

Chapped Lip Treatment

Ingredients

4 parts beeswax
4 parts castor oil
3 parts sesame oil
2 parts anhydrous lanolin

Directions

Blend all ingredients in a double boiler, blending
with a stainless steel spoon.

Chapped Hand Treatment

Ingredients

2 parts beeswax
1 part coconut oil

Directions

Melt beeswax, blend and cool.

Soap with Beeswax

Ingredients

1 and 1/2 cups clean rendered tallow
1/2 cup vegetable oil
3 tablespoons beeswax
3/4 cup cold soft water
1/4 cup lye flakes
1 teaspoon citronella oil
1/4 teaspoon lemon oil (optional)
2 tablespoons liquid honey (optional)

Directions

Melt beeswax in double boiler; beat in vegetable oil.
Melt tallow and measure. Dissolve lye flakes in cold
water, thoroughly mix lye solution with melted
tallow and add melted beeswax-vegetable oil
mixture in a thin stream beating vigorously until
thoroughly blended. Add honey, citronella and
lemon oils, blending thoroughly. Grease mold(s)
with petroleum jelly or silicone spray; pour into
mold(s). Makes 1.5 pounds hard bar soap.

Borax Skin Creams—Each column will produce a different skin cream product.

(Wong 1990)

Proportions in Grams

Ingredients											
Oil Phase											
Beeswax	8.0	10.0	8.0	10.2	12.0	4.0	12.0	16.67	5.0	16.0	14.0
Mineral Oil	49.0	57.0	56.0	54.0	56.0	39.8	50.25	50.0	54.0	48.0	52.0
Paraffin	7.0	—	—	—	—	12.0	—	—	10.0	5.0	—
Cetyl Alcohol	1.0	—	—	—	12.5	—	—	—	—	—	—
Cet. Esters Wax	—	2.0	—	10.0	—	—	—	—	—	—	—
Spermaceti	—	—	—	—	—	—	5.0	—	—	—	—
Ozokerite	—	—	10.0	—	—	—	5.0	—	—	—	—
Petrolatum	—	—	—	—	—	12.0	—	—	10.0	—	—
Lanolin	—	—	—	—	—	—	2.0	—	—	—	—
Water Phase											
Glycerin	—	—	—	—	—	—	—	—	2.0	—	—
Borax	0.4	0.7	0.6	0.8	0.5	20.2	0.75	0.83	1.0	1.0	1.0
Distilled Water	34.6	30.3	25.4	25.0	19.0	32.0	5.0	32.5	18.0	30.0	33.0

Directions

Blend and heat borax, distilled water and glycerin to 158°F (70°C). Melt beeswax to the same temperature in a separate container. Blend all together, stirring rapidly. If you care to add perfume, the blend should be allowed to cool to about 122°F (50°C) since the perfume will volatilize out of the blend at higher temperatures. The perfume should be slowly added and the blend stirred until it solidifies.

Chapter IV

Figure IV.1. Artwork with bees-wax—A Ukrainian Easter Egg.

Beeswax in Art

Beeswax casting

Beeswax has many applications in art. The ancient Greeks made their death masks by taking a likeness of the face of the deceased with plaster. Once hardened, the plaster cast was removed and used as a mold for the beeswax mask. Beeswax can be hand formed to produce some interesting items. To do this, the beeswax must be warmed by immersing it in hot water.

Beeswax is combined in equal parts with beef tallow and paraffin wax for the casting or carving of decorative figures for banquet tables.

Beeswax carving

Pure beeswax can also be carved. The ancient Greeks used beeswax extensively for making busts and statues of their gods and statesmen. In France, during the reign of Louis XIV, an artist named Antoine Benoist used beeswax extensively in portraits and in sculptures, one of which still survives in the Halls of Versailles. In more recent times, beeswax has been used in the figures in Madame Tussaud's Wax Museum in London, England. Beeswax can be colored by adding wood stain (which can be purchased in a hardware store) to the beeswax while the beeswax is in a liquid state, by adding candle dyes or by painting it.

Ukrainian Easter eggs

Beeswax is used in the dying process in the making of Ukrainian Easter eggs (Figure IV.1). This art form involves the use of beeswax to prevent the dye from fixing to the egg shell. The design is inscribed on the egg shell using a pencil. Those areas of the shell which you desire to remain dye-free are thinly coated with melted beeswax. The egg is then placed in the lightest dye, progressively waxed, dyed, dried and waxed again, going through a series of darker and darker dyes.

Although passable Ukrainian Easter eggs can be done using common Easter egg dyes or food dyes, very vibrant colored eggs can be made by using special Ukrainian Easter egg dyes. One of the most critical things in making these eggs is the egg itself. The purist recommends

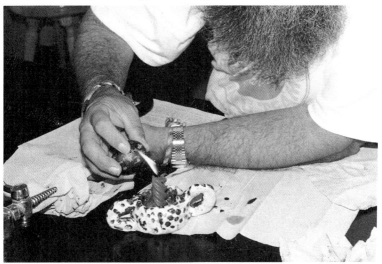

Figure IV.2. The making of Ukrainian Easter eggs is a popular subject at workshops taught by beekeeper or craft groups.

using only raw eggs. A problem in using raw eggs is that over time their contents decay, and if the egg is ever broken the very unpleasant odor of sulfur dioxide is released. It has been recommended burying the finished raw egg in cat litter. Supposedly this process takes a couple of months to draw out the obnoxious gases forming in the raw egg as its contents decay. The following methods is also used: Blow the contents out of the raw egg by punching very small holes in the top and the bottom of the egg and blowing the egg yolk and white into a dish. Since blown eggs are very difficult to submerse in the dye solutions, the blowing can be done after the dying is complete; or fill the blown egg with plaster of Paris before the dying.

I generally use a burning beeswax candle to provide the wax for waxing the egg (Figure IV.1). The egg shell is first prepared by wiping it with vinegar. The wax can be applied to the egg using a number of methods including a specially made tool called a kitska with electrically heated models now available. Tips of pencils, unwound paper clips, pen nibs, etc. can also be used. The tools are dipped in the wax pool of the candle and used to apply the liquid wax to the egg shell. Once the dying steps are completed, I gently heat the egg in the candle flame and wipe off the wax with a cloth or a paper towel (Figure IV.2).

Bavarian artwork

Another interesting use for beeswax is in Bavarian artwork. During the Middle or Dark Ages, wood carvings were common in the domiciles of nobility. The peasants, who not could afford such artwork, still wanted to emulate the well-to-do, and to accomplish this, they made carvings out of dark colored beeswax.

This type of artwork is still being done today. The beeswax is melted and then darkened to resemble the color of wood by using wood stains obtained in a hardware store. By experimenting, it is possible to get a wood grain appearance by swirling the stain into the beeswax rather than blending it completely. The stained wax can then be cast into blocks and carved, or if your carving abilities are limited, the wax can be poured into molds for various figures (see Figure X.2 on page 112). The wax figures can then be painted or very attractively colored using powdered metals such as copper, aluminum and brass which are available in many hobby shops. The powdered metals can be "painted" on by using small paint brushes or cotton swabs and further preserved by spraying the figure with clear varnish after it has been painted.

The lost wax process

The "lost wax process" involves the use of beeswax in making a master mold into which a molten metal is poured for casting. The beeswax is melted and lost in the process. The molten metal is then poured into the space once filled by wax. We recommend *Lost-Wax Casting: A Practitioner's Manual* (Feinberg 1983) for details.

Marble repair

Beeswax can also be used to preserve marble statues and other articles made of marble.[6] The preservative is made by melting together 8 parts of turpentine with 2 parts beeswax. Apply hot to the marble surfaces being sure to get it into all cracks and fissures.

Preservation

Beeswax is also used for coating paper items such as maps, documents, prints, engravings, etc. To do this, melted beeswax is thinly layered over a heated piece of plate glass. Water is then poured over the wax-coated plate glass. The document to be coated is then moistened and laid on the glass plate, covered with a piece of filter paper or paper towel and pressed down firmly. The method will impart a brilliant surface to the document.

Tree ornaments

For the Christmas season, beeswax can also be used to make very attractive Christmas tree ornaments (Figure IV.3). These ornaments can be made out of naturally colored beeswax or by dying the beeswax. The ornaments can be hand-carved or formed in various types of molds, such as those for making chocolate candy or those made of polyurethane. A loop of Christmas tree ornament hooks, fine fishing line, ribbon or cord can be used as hangers. If the ornament is going to be heavy, a sewing pin should be put through the end of the supporting ribbon to prevent the heavy ornament from pulling loose from the support. To get the ornaments to release readily from the molds, their insides can be coated with silicon spray, cooking spray, cooking oil, or talcum powder. Acrylic paints work great for painting ornaments, and Modge Podge™ or some other coating material can be applied over the paint for a semi-gloss finish.

---

[6] This method is relatively unknown to those interested in preventing further deterioration of our marble heritage, which have been damaged greatly in modern times due to air pollution and acid rain.

Figure IV.3. Easy-to-make Christmas tree ornaments may be produced from multiple molds, turning out many different ornaments in a short time.

Figure V.0. The batik designs used in this chapter, including the step-by-step series showing the development of a complex design, are the work of Pamela Marshall, Poui Designs, 3 Poui Hill, Lady Chancellor Road, Trinidad, West Indies. Her permission to photograph and reproduce these designs is greatly appreciated.

Chapter V

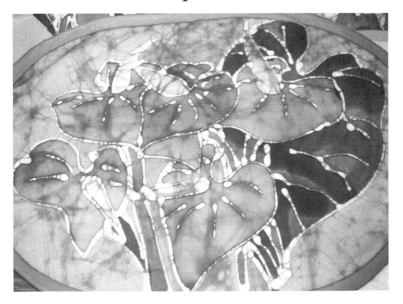

V.1. A batik pattern—made into a placemat—is an attractive display.

Batik

Margo Barraclough

Batik is a very old art form which enjoys great popularity today. It involves the dying of cloth with successively darker dyes while building up a design or pattern with a beeswax-paraffin mixture. There is a creative excitement while working on a batik project, since the final outcome is not known until the project is finished. Experience will show a wide range of techniques and results with different dyes, fabrics, applicators and wax mixtures.

Batik originated in the Orient, and many villages in Java have their own unique design. Natives use carved blocks of wood to transfer the wax, allowing a mass production/assembly line technique.

Margo Barraclough is a retired school art teacher living in Pittsburgh, Pennsylvania.

Figure V.2. A special batik tool, called a canting, holds hot wax while laying down a design.

As complicated as this may sound, I have used batik as an art project in a middle school in Pennsylvania, working with children aged 11 to 13. The children enjoy working with batik, and are very proud of their results.

I start by selecting a piece of fabric, preferably cotton, silk or linen. These fabrics take up both the wax and the dye with great success, and will give the most pleasing results. With new fabrics, be sure to remove sizing before beginning. Avoid synthetic fabrics or blends, since they do not accept the dye well.

Plan a simple composition for your initial project. I use a sunflower design when demonstrating for the children, and we put a pencil sketch lightly on the cloth. It is best to keep your plan on paper for reference. The first wax is applied to those areas where the fabric color (use white for your first project) is to be preserved. Apply the wax with a brush or a canting, the tool illustrated in Figure V.2. Be sure the wax is hot enough to penetrate the fabric, or the dye will bleed under it.

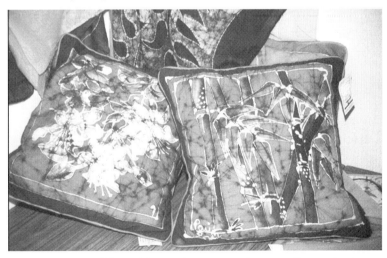

Figure V.3. By carefully building up dye on cotton, linen or silk, complex designs may be developed in the batik process.

Figure V.4. Areas which will remain the color of the fabric are covered with wax, and then dyed with the first color.

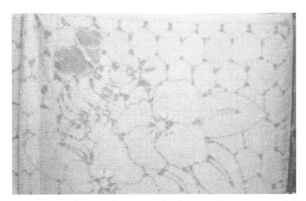

Figure V. 5. Once the initial pattern is laid down, the wax-covered fabric is put into yellow dye.

Never heat the wax directly over the heat source. Always place the wax container into a container of water to melt.

After the first wax application, the cloth is dipped into the first color and hung up to dry. Keep in mind that each color influences subsequent colors. After the fabric has dried, wax the parts of the design that retain the color of the first dye, then dip the cloth into the next color, and allow to dry. During the waxing and drying process, dry the fabric thoroughly, or the wax will not adhere to the cloth.

In the series of examples (Figures V.4-V.9) the artist has first waxed parts of the design that are to remain white, and then dyed the fabric yellow. After waxing the areas of the design to be left yellow, the

Figure V.6. The second pattern is waxed. These areas will remain yellow.

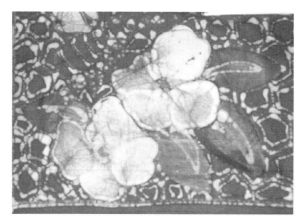

Figure V.7. The cloth is dyed in the second color

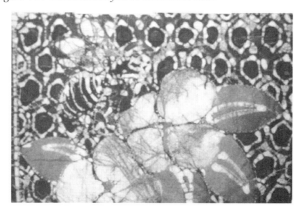

Figure V.8. More wax is added and the cloth dyed black or a dark color.

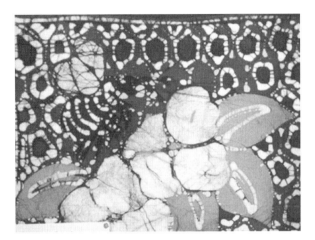

Figure V.9. The wax is ironed or boiled off to reveal the final pattern.

fabric was dipped into light blue, which resulted in a light green color. There are endless possibilities for colors, and it is not always necessary to immerse the entire project into a dye. If, for example, at some point the artist wished to add some darker green leaves or accents, he or she could wax over the areas to remain light green, and then apply darker blue or green with a brush where desired. When these areas are dry, they too can be waxed, and the next color dipped. In the case of our example, the next color is pink, which results in a purple-brown. Once the purple-brown was washed, the last color used is a dark or black dye to create the crackle effect.

I used special batik dyes available in craft stores. These give the best results. One may try cold water fabric dyes available in most supermarkets. The dyes must be usable in cold water or the wax may be softened during the dying process if heated!

Beeswax is an important part of the batik process, but should be mixed with microcrystalline paraffin to produce the proper melting temperature and degree of hardness on the fabric. Microcrystalline paraffin has a higher melting point than beeswax, but batik with pure microcrystalline paraffin may result in pieces of the wax separating from the fabric, thus loosening the pattern. Pure beeswax is too soft on the fabric, and may not give the proper edges in the design. I use a mixture of half beeswax and half microcrystalline paraffin in our projects, and have had excellent results. However, there is always room for experimentation for different effects. Pure beeswax may give a nice effect if a softer pattern is wanted.

During the final dye we scrunch the cloth to produce very fine cracks in the wax. After putting the cloth in a dark dye, this results in dark lines throughout the design, which gives the fabric the desired spider web appearance. I find that black dye creates a less desirable effect than other dark pigments. Experiment with dark browns, dark blues, purples and other saturated colors.

When the final result has been obtained, you still must remove the wax from the fabric. Since newspaper may smear printer's ink on the cloth, I use clean paper bags from the grocery store, which are flattened with any printing away from the cloth. With a hot iron, heat the cloth between layers of the grocery bags. With repeated ironing, the wax should be removed. The cloth may be laundered and framed or put to use. Some artists like to leave a residue of wax on the fabric to provide a stiffening. This is a matter of taste and desired effect.

One resource book you may find in the local library is by Noel Dyrenforth, called *The Technique of Batik* (B. T. Batsford, Ltd., London). Many other references are available.

Figure V.10. All manner of clothing, household items and wall hangings may be developed using batik.

Chapter VI

Figure VI.1. A beeswax rose is easy to make using the techniques found in this chapter.

Beeswax Flowers

Elizabeth A. Duffin

Very attractive and realistic wax flowers can be made from beeswax. One of the first records of the making of beeswax flowers is attributed to the Greek physician and botanist Dioscorides during the First Century, who, it is reported, rolled beeswax into sheets from which he made his flowers.

To make beeswax flowers you need thin sheets of wax which can be cut into either petal or leaf shapes. Flat pieces of wax can be made on a piece of plywood, while the curved pieces may be made on spoons.

Elizabeth A. Duffin is a beekeeper and artist who lives in Ringwood, Hants, England.

Wax must be very clean and free from propolis and any contamination. I use wax recovered from old combs in a solar wax extractor and then filtered through a very fine cloth in the oven or a steam wax extractor. I keep my capping wax for competitive show and fancy candles.

Remember, for safety reason, wax should always be melted in a water bath and never on direct heat. I use a shallow bowl standing in an old frying pan of water. Remember to add water to the pan if you work for any length of time.

Figure VI.2. Pour the liquid wax onto the water-soaked plywood. Multiple layers make thicker wax.

Soak a piece of plywood in a pan of cold water. Soaking the wood in water will stop the wax from sticking. Melt the wax in the water bath and add dye to get the color you require. Since natural beeswax is yellow in color, the addition of dyes may produce unexpected results. For example, the addition of blue dye to natural yellow wax will result in a shade of green. However, it will not be a deep green needed for the leaves of flowers, so add green dye to get a good green color. For blue color, you will need to used bleached beeswax and blue dye.

To pour the wax, use a piece of plywood no wider then the bowl containing the water. Shake excess water off the plywood and hold it at an angle above the

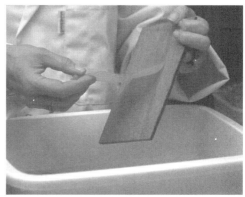

Figure VI.3. After the wax cools in a pan of water, gently peel off the wax and allow it to completely harden.

bowl of wax. With a ladle, pour the wax onto the top of the plywood letting the excess wax run back into the wax bowl. Dunk the plywood with the sheet of wax into the bowl of cold water and the sheet of wax will float off (yes, it really will!). To make thicker wax, pour another layer of wax before dunking[7]. Make as many sheets in as many colors as you require. You will need to pour test sheets to check colors when you mix the dye with the wax.

To make petals, I use spoons to provide a

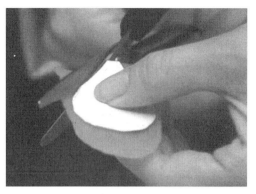

Figure VI.4. Use the pattern to cut the wax to the desired shape. Here a petal is being cut.

Figure VI.5. Use a piece of glass and a craft knife to cut delicate patterns, or if the wax is thin.

convex shape. Stand the spoons in a bowl of water into which you have added dish soap (washing up liquid). I use 1 teaspoon to 1 pint of water. The soap acts as a wetting and releasing agent. Dip the spoon into the wax tip first and then tilt the spoon to let excess wax run off by one side of the handle. Repeat once more letting the wax run off the other side of the handle. When the wax is cool, run the edge of a blunt knife around the bowl of the spoon to separate the inner and outer wax shapes. Gently ease the wax off the back of the spoon into the palm of your hand. Then remove the piece from the inside with the ball of

Figure VI.6. Use metal spoons to make curved petals, using a knife to separate the layers.

[7] Another method of making sheets of wax is to melt wax to a desired thickness in a pan of hot water. Once the wax has solidified, loosen it from the edge of the pan with a sharp knife.

Figure VI.7. Gently remove the wax on the outside of the spoon with the palm of your hand. Remove inside wax with your fingertips.

your hand. Remember, the wax is very fragile while it is still warm!

Petals can be cut to shape using a pair of scissors, a sharp knife or a razor blade. The wax from the back of the spoon is used for making a closed flower and the wax from inside the bowl of the spoon for an open flower such as a water lily, so that the best surface is the one you see in the final product.

Design and make a rose

Decide on the flower you want to make and use a real flower to make your patterns and to see how the flower is constructed. I find this

Figure VI.8. Different sized and shaped spoons will give you a wide range of useful 'petals' for your flowers.

is the only way to work. While I give you patterns for a rose and a water lily at the end of this chapter, I think you will have much better results if you base your pattern on a real flower, and make comparisons as you assemble and shape the flower. Make

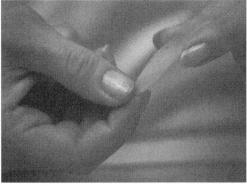

Figure VI.9. Use your fingers to form the petal into the desired shape.

your pattern by taking a flower apart and tracing

the pattern. Cut out the shapes in wax by using either a pair of scissors or craft knife with the wax on a piece of glass.

All stemmed flowers are started in the same way. Take a small amount of a cotton ball (cotton wool) and twist it around the end of a piece of florist's wire for about an inch, then fold the top inch of wire over to anchor the cotton in place.

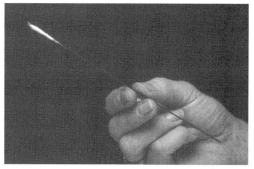

Figure VI.10. Twist a small amount of cotton around the end of a florist's wire and then fold the top inch of wire over to anchor the cotton in place.

Wrap the wire with florist's binding tape starting at the cotton end and covering part of the cotton. Then dip the cotton into melted beeswax. This knob of cotton and wax will stop the flower head from falling off the wire. For the center of the rose, push the wire through the center of the wax circle up to the cotton knob. Fold the circle in half and then in half again, pressing firmly on the folds.

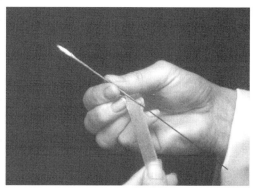

Figure VI.11. Bind the florist's wire with floral tape.

Roll the center so the curved edges give the effect of petals unfurling. Squeeze the wax

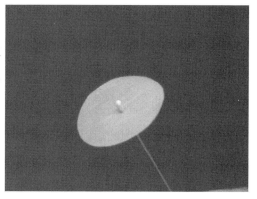

Continued on page 62

Figure VI.12. Insert wire in center of the wax circle and fold around the cotton to form the center.

Figures VI.13 to VI.18. Top left: Fold wax circle in half. Top right: Fold wax again to form a quarter of the original circle. Middle left: Wrap wax around wire to form the center of the flower. Middle right: Form edge of wax to resemble an opening petal. Bottom left: Add the first petal, carefully attaching the base of the petal to the base of the developing flower. Working at room temperature, the warmth of your fingers will warm the wax enough to fasten each petal securely. Bottom right: Attach additional petals, working carefully to duplicate the position of the petals as found in the real flower you are using as a model.

Figures VI.19 to VI.24. Top left: Continue adding petals to complete the flower. Top right: When all the petals have been added, push the wire through the center of the septal and fasten to the base of the flower. Middle left: Attach a small piece of green wax to form the base or 'hip' of the flower. Middle right: Wrap a piece of florist's wire with florist's tape and sandwich between two identical pieces of green wax to form the leaf. Bottom left: Fasten a thin piece of wire three-quarters of an inch below the leaf. Attach two side leaves to the wire. Bottom right: Attach the finished leaf to the stem of the flower and position into a lifelike shape.

onto the wire just below the cotton. Working in a warm room the warmth of your fingers will be sufficient to soften the wax. Using a real rose or a photograph as a guide you are now ready to attach the petals. These should be shaped by pressing the center of the petal with the ball of your thumb and then curving back the edges of the petals to give a good shape. Attach them one at a time to the wire, each time so that the petals adhere firmly. When the rose is the size you want, slide the calyx up to the base of the rose, pushing it up close to the petals and squeezing it into place. Press scraps of wax below the calyx to form the 'hip'.

Leaves may be cut from two sheets of wax together. Bind a piece of florist's wire with tape and sandwich this between the two layers of the top leaf. Twist a piece of thin wire around the stem three-quarters of an inch below the top leaf and sandwich the side leaves onto this wire. The rose stem can then be bound with tape again and the leaves attached at the same time.

Figure VI.25.An attractive table display of water lilies.

Figure VI.26. Form a one-inch wax base and fasten four large petals while the wax is still warm.

Figure VI.27. Fasten the second set of petals to the base.

Figure VI.28. Fasten both sets of small petals to the base, but do not fold the petals into final shape.

Water lily

Use convex petals made on the inside of a metal table (dessert) spoon and a teaspoon. Eight petals of each size are required to make a water lily.

Since the stems of water lilies are not visible, use a disk of beeswax about an inch in diameter and one-eighth of an inch thick. This can be made by dipping a piece of one-inch dowel, soaked in water, into the molten beeswax until it is the required thickness. While this disk is still warm and soft, the prepared petals can be pressed firmly into place. Four large petals first pressed onto the edge of the disk, windmill fashion, four more large petals set further in and between the first four, and then the eight small petals can be added in the same way. Stamen can be made using lengths of cotton thread or fine string dipped into molten beeswax and then pressed into the center of the flower. The small petals can then be gently curled upwards to

Figure VI.29. Duplicate the pistils (center of flower) with small pieces of wax; dip threads in wax to form the filaments and anthers.

give a more natural effect. Lily pads can be cut from sheets of beeswax to make an attractive display which could be used as a table decoration.

These are just a few ideas to get you going. Have a go at beeswax flower making. Who knows what you can produce if you try!

Materials in this chapter were adapted from materials ©1988 by Elizabeth A. Duffin.

Figure VI.30. Carefully fasten pistils and anthers in the center of the flower and position petals.

Figure VI.31. Cut the leaf from a wax sheet, and make the stem from wrapped florist's tape.

Figure VI.32. Welcome spring with crocus flowers made from beeswax.

Figure VI.33. Columbine flowers can look just like the real thing.

Figure VI.34. Christmas cactus complete with plant stake to fool your friends!

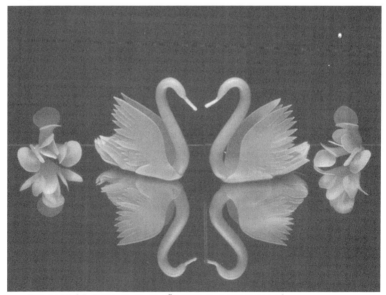

Figure VI.35. Beeswax swans floating on a mirror pond.

Rose Patterns

Figure VI.36. Patterns for making a rose. Top left is a rose petal. Top right is the center of the flower. On the bottom is the star-like calyx.

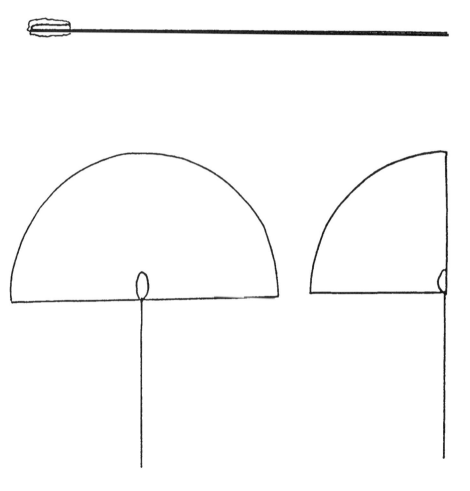

Figure VI.37. Using florist's wire and a bit of cotton, wrap the center of the flower around the cotton, fold, and roll, begin to apply petals.

Figure VI. 38. The leaf of the rose is made of florist's wire, florist's tape and the wax leaves.

Water Lily Patterns

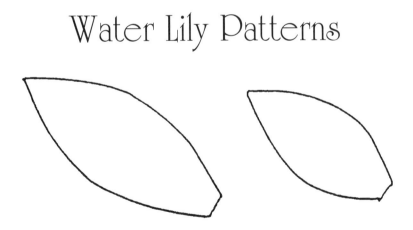

Figure VI. 39. Patterns for making the water lily described in this chapter.

Figure VII.0. A sample of encaustic painting, showing the range of expression this medium offers. From Bob Berthold's collection.

Chapter VII

Figure VII.1. Simple landscape formed by using the four basic effects produced by encaustic wax and the painting iron. By Michael Bossom.

Encaustic Art

Encaustic: To burn in

Michael Bossom

A brief history

As long ago as 400 B.C., naturally available beeswax was being mixed with pigments and used as a painting medium. Long before oil paints were developed and introduced, encaustic techniques, requiring a heat source to render the wax paint liquid, were being used to create artworks. In the beginning were cave paintings—earth colors smeared onto the walls of our ancestors' homes or perhaps their sacred places. These records of the animal life of their age remain today. It is generally

---

Michael Bossom is a commercial artist living in Glogue, Wales. Text and artwork include new and previously published materials © by Michael Bossom

accepted that encaustic wax paints bridged the gap between the first visual expressions raw from the earth and laid the foundation which took painting from a mural activity into the realm of easel painting.

The Ancients of Greece, Rome and Egypt used a simple method for their work. A heated palette, warmed over a charcoal fire, was used to create an environment suitable for holding the colors in a liquid state. The mixtures seem to have consisted of pigment blended with beeswax and resins. Most authorities accept that dammar resin (a varnish derived from trees) or shellac were used with the wax in order to raise the melting point and create a harder surface than the beeswax would naturally offer. These molten colored wax mixtures were then applied by brush to a rigid surface. Thin boards of wood were certainly used as support for the portraiture that remains from this period.

Stiff brushes were not the only means of applying and manipulating waxes. The Romans used a tool referred to as a *cestrum* which seems to have been like a heavy bronze palette knife. It has been recorded that in France the body of a female encaustic painter was found surrounded by her materials and *cauteria*. This report indicates that the tool—a *cautarium* resembled a long fine spoon and might have been used to ladle the wax colors onto horizontal works. It is pure assumption then as to how more detailed lines and marks were achieved but perhaps several methods of working were combined in order to accomplish desired results.

In classical terms, it is considered as the true mark of an encaustic painting that it should be 'burned in'. This involves melting the whole surface of the finished work to create a single final surface where all the various applications of colored wax become melted together, yet without disturbance of the painted image. This produces a consistent single surface affording protection to the pigments and allowing a final burnishing of the work. Encaustic works need no fixing and are not especially attractive to dust, so once softly polished the waxes simply reveal their natural and gentle glossy sheen.

Examples of portraiture have been found in many Egyptian tombs in excellent condition. The portraits from Fayum are good examples of the style in which the Ancients worked. Several examples can be seen in Room 64 at the British Museum in London. These portraits dramatically display the durability inherent in encaustic paint. Beeswax, it seems, lasts a very long time!

Various revivals usually concerned with mural techniques have quietly come and gone. Not so surprising when oil paints, tempera, water color and now acrylics and resins are so available and accepted. Who wants to light a fire in order to start painting? But a new potential has emerged and now electrically heated tools are readily available and affordable. Heat as a solvent suddenly offers whole new possibilities. At the flick of a switch paintings can be reworked. Creatively many effective techniques and methods can be employed to achieve results simply unattainable by the more conventionally accepted evaporating solvents. So now we have a chance and a challenge, the opportunity to revive this most ancient and respected medium which, united with modern technology, invites a new exploration of its possibilities. And this work, if carefully developed, will last a long time. Indeed, a very long time.

Encaustic wax

Paint is a mixture consisting of a solid pigment suspended in a liquid, that, when applied to a surface, dries to form a hard coating. Many different mediums are used as the suspension agent for pigment—oil, water, etc. All these mediums use evaporation as the mechanism for change from liquid form to a solid state. However, wax does not need to rely on that concept but offers the alternative use of heat as the solvent.

Beeswax melts at around 60°C (150°F). Encaustic waxes may contain several ingredients but are normally designed to melt around 70°C (160°F). There are a number of waxes which add certain properties to encaustic painting:

Natural Beeswax—is naturally a yellowish color. Bleached beeswax will also yellow through time.
Carnauba wax—comes from the leaves of a Brazilian palm tree (wax palm) and has both a higher melting point and a harder composition than beeswax. When used as an ingredient it adds these qualities to the resultant encaustic medium.
Microcrystalline wax—can be added to soften the encaustic medium.
Dammar resin—another tree-derived product. This resin adds toughness to encaustic medium and raises the melting point.

Classical mixtures for producing encaustic wax paint medium usually advise not less than 70% beeswax because it is the most durable component. As modern chemistry reveals and develops other potentials, new materials may emerge. All encaustic mediums are prepared by combining the ingredients through the condition of low heat. If excessive heat is applied some breakdown of the materials may occur so it is vital not to use excessive heat. Avoid temperatures over 100°C (212°F).

The classical mixture for encaustic wax medium is considered to be about 85% natural beeswax combined through low heat with 15% dammar resin. Perhaps rather than using a resin, replace the dammar with 10-15% carnauba wax. If this is too hard or brittle for your usage, reduce the percentage or introduce some proportion of microcrystalline wax.

Pigments which have been suitably ground can then be added to the medium. Some pigments are dangerous when heated so take care when

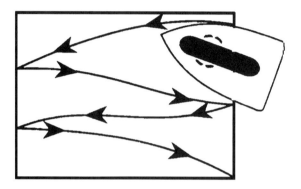

Figure VII.2. Use enough wax, smooth gently and zig-zag down the card, but DON'T PRESS TOO HARD.

choosing materials. A range of non-toxic encaustic art waxes and dyes are available and advised for experimenting with the methods that follow this section.

Start being creative

Using encaustic waxes (light-fast, non-toxic pigments) and a low temperature electric painting iron, these basic methods describe how to spread, dab and generally manipulate the colored waxes by working onto an encaustic painting card. The encaustic card base enables the waxes to be moved around and re-worked until a satisfactory result emerges. Since heat is the solvent for the wax, a new image is formed every time the warmed painting iron touches the waxed card. Through these simple techniques, everyone, no matter what their painting skill, has the opportunity to create exciting, colorful and almost instant images without too much effort! Making greeting cards is very reward-ing while landscapes and abstracts stretch your imagination and de-velop skills. The possibilities are endless. Heat is the solvent. Any part of the encaustic artwork can be changed at any time.

Figure VII.3. Random zig-zag smoothing pattern.

What do you need?

To get started you will need to assemble encaustic waxes and an encaustic painting card (which must at least have a high quality non-absorbent surface). Start with small sizes. Also have some clean disposable paper, such as unprinted newsprint or computer paper, and soft household tissues for cleaning the iron and polishing your results. You will need an electric painting iron. The "Encaustic Art Painting Iron" is designed for this use and will enable excellent results. Some household and travel irons can also be used when set at "COOL" but any coatings must be removed from the base using fine abrasive paper. Do not use a steam iron, unless you want psychedelic clothes. It is best to keep your iron just for painting!

Basic iron work

There are four basic types of effect that the iron easily produces but first check that the temperature of the iron is correctly set. Take some encaustic wax and gently press it against the surface of the iron where it should slowly melt. If it doesn't the iron is too cold and the thermostat

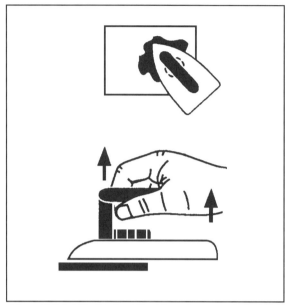

Figure VII.4. Lift off—fast! Do this action several times on the same wax and card.

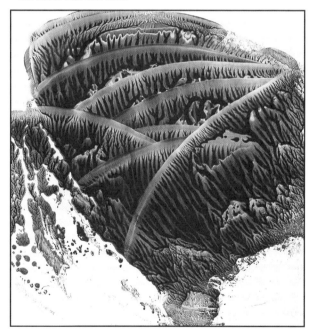

Figure VII.5. Lifting or dabbling marks left by the iron.

should be turned to a slightly hotter setting. When the iron with molten wax is raised to a vertical position the wax color should very slowly dribble down the iron. If it moves quickly and appears more like water than a thick oily liquid, the iron may be too hot. The wax should behave as a sticky molten liquid rather than cold cooking oil.

1. Smoothing

Place a small piece of encaustic painting card on the clean work area, then load a good amount of a dark colored encaustic wax onto the iron. Now turn the iron face down and gently smooth the wax back and forth across the card working towards the bottom (see Figure VII.2). Make sure to use enough wax and don't press too hard. You should get something along the lines of Figure VII.3.

2. Lifting or dabbing

Take another card and load the iron with wax again. This time put the iron down on the middle of the card and then remove it by using a fast lifting-off action (See Figure VII.4). Do this several times without applying any further wax, placing the iron down in a slightly different area each time. The results will be something like Figure VII.5. The liquid wax has caused a suction to develop between the card and the iron which is now broken. These marks are caused by in-rushing air splitting the wax into channels. This is an exciting and very useful effect.

3. Edge strokes

Smear more wax onto another piece of card with the base of the iron and then turn the iron on its edge (Figure VII.6). Move the iron through the wax, following the narrowest edge and keep in line rather like an ice-skate on ice. You should get thin lines but if you move the iron sideways it will behave more like a snow plow and create wider, thicker lines (see Figure VII.7).

4. Using the point of the iron

The point of the iron can be used to apply smaller and finer amounts of wax onto the card surface. Dip the point directly into a block of wax. Using this loaded point make small marks and lines on a piece of painting card. The iron can be held as you find most comfortable (See Figure VII.8). Various results from drawing with the point are illustrated in Figure VII.9.

These four types of mark-making are the foundation of modern encaustic painting with an iron. By combining these effects in different ways, many exciting and pleasing images can be formed.

Figure VII.6. Left: Iron on edge seen from behind. Right: Iron on edge seen from left end of the table.

Figure VII.7. Thin edge used like an ice skate gives a thin line. Push forward and sideways like a snow plow for thicker lines.

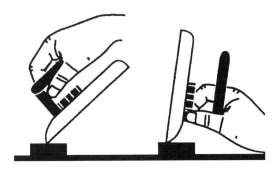

Figure VII.8. For point work, hold the iron whichever way is easiest. Resting your forearm on the table gives more control.

Figure VII.9. Various small marks from point of the iron. For birds, place loaded tip on the card, flick right and lift off. Then put tip back to start, flick left and lift off. Too much wax gives heavy, indistinct marks.

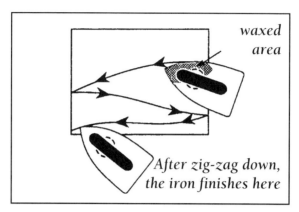

Figure VII.10. Load the iron as shown with plenty of wax, then spread the wax onto the card, *but don't press down hard.* Slide the iron very lightly.

Basic techniques for creating a simple landscape

These four effects can now be combined to form a very simple landscape. Smoothing with a light ironing motion is ideal for the simple creation of hills and landscapes. The dabbing techniques produce wonderful and intricate effects which occur as the iron is lifted off the waxed card, offering detailed foliage and fantasy results. This enables even non-painters to instantly achieve detailed work. Thin lines produced from the use of the iron's edge are perfect for grasses while the point work can introduce the first level of controlled graphics, *e.g.* dots of color for flowers, birds, etc.

Step 1. (Figure VII.10). Load the iron as shown with plenty of wax, then spread the wax onto the card, but don't press down hard. Slide the iron very lightly!

Step 2. (Figure VII.11). Hold the top of the card down with your free hand and place the iron on the lower half of the wax effects just created. Now lift the iron off with a few quick movements.

Step 3. Use the rounded edge of the iron as practiced in Figure VII.7. Push gently forward like a ice skate cutting through ice to achieve fine grass-like lines.

Step 4. As shown in Figure VII.8, use the top of the iron to put in finer details like a bird or some different colored flowers. Don't put too much wax onto the tip of the iron!

Practice this simple landscape on small pieces of card until you start to become familiar with the effects. Working quickly and boldly is better than fiddling about. Lightly polish the finished work when it is cool,

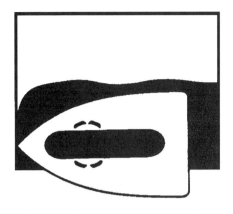

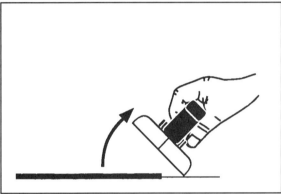

Figures VII.11 and VII.12. Hold the top of the card down with your free hand and place the iron on the lower half of the wax effects just created. Now lift the iron off with a few quick movements.

using a soft tissue pad. Encaustic artwork does not need to be fixed in any way. It can be framed open to the atmosphere with only the risk of getting scratched. However, if framed behind glass, wax artworks should not be placed in direct sunlight.

Other techniques and tools

Encaustic art is extremely versatile. The techniques already outlined illustrate a very simple approach but this wax medium offers potentials far beyond the realism of normal painting. These include drawing with heated pens and brushes, scribing and scraping through the wax like a scraper board or for deeper carving into thicker wax deposits. Building up thick deposits will add texture and relief. Blowing the colored waxes with hot air to melt and move the medium without physical contact will create special effects. Using conventional stiff brushes and either working from the upturned iron (the encaustic art painting iron converts into a small palette), or working on larger pieces using a full-sized heated palette and melting greater amounts of colored wax in suitable metal containers.

The waxes can be applied in numerous ways to fabric and absorbent materials and will withstand hard washing. Use them in one of these methods: as a resist to water color; as crayons by using abrasive action; as a liquid dissolved in turpentines or white spirit; in conjunction with oil paint (both dissolved under turps, white spirit, etc.). The list goes on and on.

There is an excellent 57-minute video by Michael Bossom made in 1992. It is packed with encaustic techniques and stimulating examples. Starting from a complete beginners point of view and steadily developing and teaching a course of progressive techniques clearly and carefully. Frequent examples inspire viewers with a sense of exploration and the confidence "to have a go".

Encaustic art using beeswax as the vital component is one of humankind's oldest and most proven color mediums and will continue to move and grow in the future. It is durable, re-workable, creative and outstandingly versatile.

For further information on encaustic art supplies and the developing work of Michael Bossom contact:

Gayle Cronin, Arts Encaustic International
8309 Mondon Way
Orangevale, CA 95662
Phone 916-726-7567
or
Michael Bossom
Glogue, Dyfed, Wales SA36 0ED
Phone from United States: (011-44) 239 831401;
from U.K. (0239) 831401

Chapter VIII

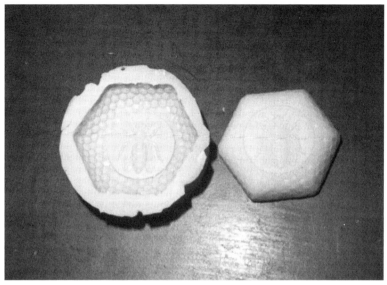

Figure VIII.1 Small cakes of beeswax may be used in the kitchen, workshop, sewing box and fishing tackle box. They are easily molded in a variety of forms.

Home Uses For Beeswax

Lubricant

Beeswax makes an excellent lubricant. It can be applied to sticky drawers, doors, windows, and anything else which involves sliding parts. It can be rubbed on sewing thread, fishing line, bow strings and zippers. A small amount may be put on screws, nails and pegs to facilitate their driving.

Cookie sheets and irons

Beeswax can be put on the surfaces of hot cleaned cookie sheets and clothes irons to produce non-stick surfaces. The beeswax is rubbed on the hot surface and then any excess is wiped off.

Wood filler

After keeping bees for a number of years, you will find that you have chunks of beeswax ranging in color from light yellow to black. By matching colors and warming the wax, it can be used as a wood filler and also for filling the space over counter-sunk screws and nails. Beeswax can also be colored by using oil based stains, producing a filler that approximates the color of the wood being filled. When we added an addition to our home we used beeswax extensively for patching, covering and finishing the wood paneled walls. We also used beeswax to "grout" cracks where we replaced a section of oak flooring.

Polish

I had my first experience in making beeswax polish long before I was aware that anyone else had experimented with this. At the time I had serious intentions of marrying the young lady that I was dating (and whom I later did marry), and I decided to make her a hope chest. Upon completion of the chest, I thought that it should be finished with a beeswax polish. I combined 90% beeswax with 10% turpentine. It took me more time to apply the beeswax polish than it did to make the hope chest. It is interesting to note that the hope chest still resides in our bedroom, and that it has never needed another coat of wax after 25 years.

Figure VIII.2. Furniture polish and creams can be easily made from beeswax, and will serve many purposes.

In addition to turpentine, a number of other materials can be blended with beeswax to make polishes. Some people find the smell of turpentine quite irritating. For this reason, lemon oil can be substituted for the turpentine.

The use of this polish will impart an excellent and extremely durable gloss on just about any surface that will support a wax finish. We have used this polish to finish woodworking projects without the use of any type of varnish or shellac. We have waxed furniture and found the resultant finish to be resistant to water and other liquids. We have used it on wood paneling and other places, again with fine results.

The polish is also an excellent way to protect tools from rusting. Before applying the polish, the tools should be completely free of grease, oil, dirt and rust.

Many craftsmen who restore antique woodenware use beeswax polishes of varying compositions to refinish their items, and these same formulations can be successfully used on waxing any wooden item. In all instances, ingredients should be blended in a double boiler and stored in wide-mouth screw-top containers.

To produce an easy-to-apply paste-wax (unlike my hope chest polish), melt approximately equal parts of beeswax and turpentine, or other desired wax solvent, keeping in mind that these substances are highly flammable and therefore should be heated in a double boiler with an electric heat source as opposed to a flame. Blend them thoroughly and pour into a wide-mouth screw-top container for storage and use.

Liquid furniture polish

Ingredients

1 part beeswax
4 parts distilled turpentine
1 part high quality liquid soap
2 parts water (use soft or lime-free water)

Scratched furniture polish

Ingredients

1 part beeswax
1 part naphtha
1 part boiled linseed oil

Cream furniture polish

Ingredients

1 part beeswax
1 part high quality liquid soap
1 part pine oil
8 parts distilled turpentine
4 parts hot water (use soft or lime-free water)

Furniture polish

Ingredients

1 part beeswax

1 part naphtha
1 part raw linseed oil

Furniture polish

Ingredients

1 part beeswax
1 part linseed oil

Leather preparation

An excellent preparation for treating and waterproofing leather can be made by melting together 1 part beeswax, 1 part beef tallow (tallow is rendered beef fat and it is obtainable from rendering plants and possibly from butcher shops or fast food restaurants), and 1 part neats-foot oil (obtainable in many hardware or horse supply stores). The electric hot plate-double boiler method should be used in making the

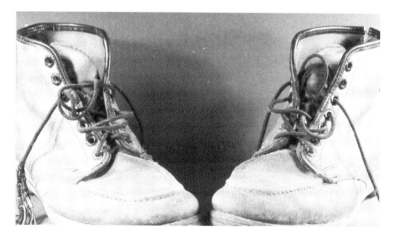

Figure VIII.3. Beeswax may be blended with other materials to produce a high quality treatment for leather.

beeswax leather preparation. We have been using this preparation on our leather hunting boots and have found it to restore "life" to the scuffed and worn leather, as well as being an effective waterproofing product. Each year the members of our college beekeeping club make a jar of this product for themselves and they have not only used it on leather footwear but on leather jackets, leather upholstery and leather ridding tack (Figure VIII.3).

Metal protection

Pure beeswax and beeswax combined with other agents protects iron and steel and certain other metals, imparting to their surfaces a strong resistance to corrosion. The corrosion (oxidation) of the metal can be prevented by heating the metal item in melted beeswax heated to at least 180°F (86°C). The item should be allowed to remain in the beeswax until its temperature reaches that of the wax When the item is lifted out, all but a thin film of wax should remain on it. We have had steel screws treated with beeswax outdoors for a number of years without any sign of rust.

Temporary adhesive

Since beeswax adheres readily to many materials, it can be used to temporarily hold lightweight things together until they can be permanently attached. For example, it can be used to hold parts of models together until they can be glued. It can also be used to hold fine wires together in electrical work until they can be soldered.

Marble repair

A mixture of resin, plaster of Paris and beeswax can be combined by heating and mixing in a double boiler.

Marble repair compound

8 parts resin
4 parts plaster of Paris
1 part beeswax

Combine by heating and mix in a double boiler. Broken pieces of marble can then be rejoined by cleaning the opposing surfaces with a stiff wire brush, heating them gently with a blow torch, and applying the compound to the surfaces before rejoining them.

Marble seal

8 parts turpentine
2 parts beeswax

This mixture of turpentine and beeswax is excellent for sealing the surface of statues. The mixture should be melted and rubbed hot onto the surface of the statue, taking care to get it into all cracks and fissures.

Plant grafting wax

Beeswax can be used to make grafting wax equal to or better than anything available commercially. Warm and hand knead equal parts of tallow (sources mentioned in section on leather preparation, page 86), rosin and beeswax.

Tree wounds

When mowing and doing other yard work, I sometimes hit a tree or shrub injuring some of the bark. Open plant wounds serve as a place for insects and plant diseases to easily enter the plant. These wounds can be effectively closed by painting either melted beeswax or grafting wax over the wound.

Leaky canvas

For many years we have gone tent camping. Vacations always have their share of rainy days, and tent canvas has a habit of developing leaks right over where you are trying to sleep! We found that a number of the beeswax preparations such as that for leather, furniture polish and grafting, work quite well in waterproofing a leaky spot in canvas. Mark where the leak is and then apply one of the wax compounds externally to it when the canvas is dry.

Sail making

Sail makers use a blend of beeswax, rosin and paraffin (wax or oil) to treat their twine. This greatly extends the life of the twine, even in the presence of harsh salt water, by combining with and waterproofing the fibers of the twine. The blend has a further advantage in that it makes it easier to draw the twine through the canvas.

Fine sewing

In fine hand sewing, the thread is passed over a small block of beeswax to give the thread better handling ability and suppleness.

Chapter IX

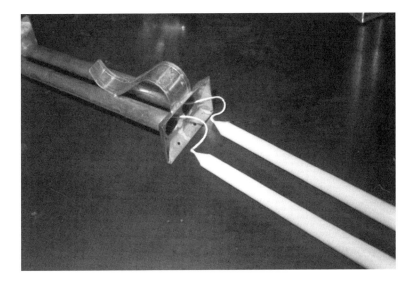

Figure IX.1 Tapered candles from metal molds are traditionally used for table decoration. They add an elegant touch.

Making Candles

Beeswax candles burn longer than those made out of most types of paraffin, and they also produce a pleasant aroma. You can use them as decorative items or they make much appreciated gifts. We have found a ready market for beeswax candles with the general public. Well crafted candles sell at premium prices in gift and novelty shops.

Candle safety

Burning candles should never be left unattended, even for a few moments. Before the use of electric Christmas tree lights, small candles were often used to light trees, resulting in many serious fires. Candles usually burn quite predictably, but from time to time they will "violate" this. During my writing of this book, a local Catholic church was completely destroyed by a fire caused by an offering candle. Over the years, the constant burning of candles had dried out the wood and finally the heat from the candles caused it to ignite. We also had another church partly damaged by a candle-started fire, and an unattended candle in one of our college dorm rooms started a fire which completely destroyed the dorm. In our home, we also had an unattended candle throw off a spark which burned a hole through a fancy lace tablecloth. Do be careful when burning candles.

Preparing the wax

In order to produce a top quality candle that burns cleanly with a minimum of dripping (guttering), sputtering and smoking, make sure the wax is completely free of contaminants such as honey, pollen and propolis. These contaminants can be so finely distributed in the wax that they are not visible to the naked eye. The propolis problem can be eliminated by using unstained capping wax. When propolis (a natural resin collected by bees from tree buds) is present in the wax, it will cause a leaf-like carbon deposit to form at the burning tip of the wick. This carbon deposit can cause an afterglow when the candle is extinguished, and if the candle is blown out, the deposit can fly off, soiling and/or

burning whatever it lands on. The honey and pollen problems can be eliminated by washing the cappings with cool water. The use of hot water can cause the incorporation of honey and pollen in the wax.

For many years, I never knew from batch to batch whether the candles we made would gutter (drip) or not. An old-time beekeeper/candlemaker shared with me his secret of relatively dripless candles. He boiled the beeswax, no matter how

Figure IX.2. Tapered tube candle molds have been used for hundreds of years. Use new molds: antique molds often have deteriorated to the point that they are no longer functional.

clean it looked, in lime-free water for at least 10 minutes (before trying this, read comments on page 30). We have been doing this ever since with great results. The boiled wax is removed from the heat and allowed to sit for about 10 minutes, to allow any water vapor in it to escape. At this point, we pour the wax through some type of clean filtering material (sweat-suit material with the fiber side up seems to work best, as shown in Figure II.4), and the wax is then ready for candlemaking. Be sure not to let your blocks of wax rest on any dirty surface because beeswax acts as a "magnet" for dirt particles.

Commercial beekeepers who produce high quality beeswax use different methods to produce their wax. One may produce honey in combs placed over a queen excluder. If the combs are white, and have not had brood reared in them, the capping wax will be quite light in color. Other commercial beekeepers melt wax in a large vat and maintain it in a liquid state for 12 hours. Heavier contaminants tend to sink to the bottom and lighter contaminants float to the surface. The best quality wax is drawn out from the center of the tank. These producers only use stainless steel equipment to prevent color changes in the wax.

Wicking

Due to its weaving and chemical treatment, commercially made candle wicking should be used instead of string. The type and size of the wicking needed varies with the diameter of the candle and also to some degree to the individual batch of beeswax itself. Due to variations in beeswax, experiment with different sized wicking if your candles do not burn to your satisfaction. If the wick is too thin, it will either extinguish itself or cause the candle to gutter or drip. If the wick is too thick, the candle will burn too rapidly and possibly smoke. To control candle burning, many churches use "burners", which are glass or metal caps which sit on the top of the candle with the wick protruding.

Braided or plaited wicking improves candle burning because the wick bends slightly at the tip during burning, thus extending it into the air current which surrounds the candle. The wick requirements of free standing candles are different for candles in bottles, where the air flow properties are different. In bottle candles, the wick should stand straight and will produce a carbon cap. This cap increases the wax-melting area. Wicking is often pickled, a special process which reduces 'after-glow' after a candle has been put out. During pickling, the wick is soaked in different solutions of mineral salts.

Many wicking types are available to the candlemaker, including flat braid, square braid, stranded, twisted, metal core, glass fiber, hollow and many others. Wicking may be made of a number of different materials.It is also available in many sizes, with different thread sizes. For dipping candle,s try a 30-ply wick, which is made from three strands of 10 threads each of No. 24 size thread. Square braid wicking is often used with candles made from beeswax. There are different wick manufacturers worldwide.

Beeswax has a much higher viscosity than paraffin wax, so use a higher wick count. Even a small amount of beeswax in a paraffin candle will require the use of a thicker wick.

Melting wax

Since melted wax is highly flammable, extreme caution should be exercised in handling it. I suggest you use an electric hot plate or an electric stove as a heat source rather than an open flame when melting your wax. Except where otherwise specified, your candle wax should be melted in a container placed in a hot water bath (Figure IX.3). I generally allow the water to reach the boiling point while using a candy thermometer in the melted wax to determine when it has reached the proper temperature for pouring. I recommend 180° to 185°F for metal molded candles, so when the candles cool they will contract from the sides of the mold hence expediting their removal (Figure IX.6). I pour the wax in the polyurethane molds as soon as it has melted (Figure IX.10).

Molded candles

Beeswax candles can be molded using a variety of different molds including metal, glass, plaster of Paris, polyurethane, silicone rubber and plastic.

Figure IX.3.Use an electric hot plate rather than an open flame to melt wax. Here an old coffee pot in a pan of water is used to melt wax. Use heat-proof gloves to handle the pot!

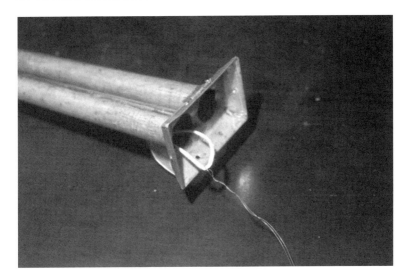

Figure IX.4. Use a thin wire to thread the wick into the candle mold.

• **Tapered Tube Molds**

Tapered tube candle molds have been used for hundreds of years. Antique molds of this type can sometimes be found, but often they have deteriorated to the point that they are no longer functional. Reproductions of these antique molds, which make perfect candles, are available (Figure IX.2). In the making of standard 10-1/2 inch high 7/8-inch diameter base tapered candles, 2/0 (30 ply) square braided wicking plus wax cleaned by the method discussed, will usually produce relatively dripless candles. To help insure easy removal of the candles, the inside of the molds should be sprayed from time to time with a good grade of silicone spray. Cooking oil, cooking spray or silicon and baby powder mixtures can also be used, but they must

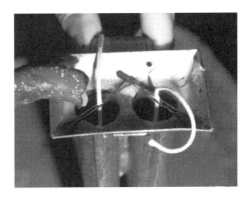

Figure IX.5. Grasp both the one-inch wick extensions and tautly support each wick down the center of each of the tubes using bobby pins or hair clips.

they don't work as well as the silicone. Also, to expedite candle removal from the mold, the wax should be heated in a double boiler for 10 minutes and poured into the mold when it is between 180° and 185°F (14-16°C). Once the wax has hardened in the mold, the mold may be placed in a freezer for about 30 minutes. This causes the wax to shrink back from the sides of the mold, making candle release easier. It may also cause a hollow core in the candle.

Bobby pins or hair clips are an excellent tool to use to suspend the wick in the molds. A 3/4-inch thick piece of household sponge cut to fit the base of the mold and dampened with cold water works well in preventing the liquid wax from escaping the tips of the mold tubes. Working on some type of kitchen tray or cookie sheet also accommodates any drips or spills.

While the wax is melting, cut the wicking into pieces long enough to extend down one tube of the mold, across the bottom, and up the second tube with approximately an extra inch of wicking extending above the top of each tube.

• Threading the Wick

Wicking can be easily threaded through the tubes by taking a piece of thin, relatively stiff wire (such as that used in reinforcing foundation in bee hive frames) and twisting a loop in one end and tightly twisting the two cut ends together using a pair of pliers. The wire can then easily be threaded through the tube, threaded through the loop, and then pulled through the tube with the wire.

Thread the second tube in the same manner, making sure that at least one inch of wicking extends above the top of the two candle mold tubes (Figure IX.4).

Another technique is to pre-wax the wick, making it stiff. The stiff wick may then be inserted into the mold without difficulty.

Grasp both

Figure IX.6. As the wax cools, it contracts in all directions. Additional wax must be added to fill the core.

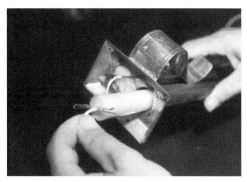

Figure IX.7. Once the wax has hardened and contracted from the sides of the metal molds, the candle may be pulled out.

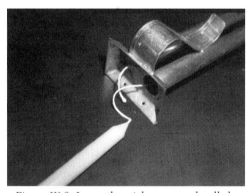

Figure IX.8. Leave the wick uncut and pull the candle out of the mold and then cut the wick, allowing you to repour the candle without rewicking!

of the one-inch wick extensions and tautly support each wick down the center of each of the tubes using bobby pins (Figure IX.5). Now place the cold water-dampened sponge on the drip tray. Place the base of the candle mold directly on the sponge, press the mold firmly down on the sponge, and pour the melted beeswax just to the top of each tube. (Some people have filled the mold completely to the rim, only to find it was more difficult to remove the candles and to trim their bases). The cool damp sponge causes the hot wax to solidify in the tips of the tubes, preventing the remaining liquid wax from escaping from around the wicking. The tray will catch any drips and the occasional leakage of wax around the sponge.

After a minute or so, the wax will solidify in the tips of the tubes and the mold can be lifted off the sponge and set on the tray. The wax will contract as it cools in the tubes. As this occurs, the tubes have to be re-topped with more melted wax to fill the cavity forming around the wick (Figure IX.7). This may have to be repeated two or three times to produce a candle with a solid base.

Once you have completed pouring and the wax has begun to harden, the bobby pins can be removed and the excess wax above the tops of the tapered tubes can be scraped off while it is still soft.

One of the most time consuming things in candlemaking is the wicking of the molds. From this standpoint, we fell in love with the

Continues on page 98

Large-Scale Candle Production

Commercial candle companies use mass-production methods to produce candles. One of the most common is the extruded candlemaking system, which forces soft wax into an extruder, producing a continuous line of candles.

A smaller production system is shown on these two pages. Located on the King of Thailand's demonstration farm in Bangkok, it allows for the production of 60 candles in each batch. The wick feeds from below (Figure IX.a, above). Liquid wax is poured into the molds, and allowed to set (Figure IX.b, right top). Once the wax has cooled, the candles are hand-cranked upward, permitting the operator to pour of the next set of candles (Figure IX.c, right bottom). The candles are then bundled into packages.

polyurethane molds because long lengths of wick can be used, and as each candle is pulled from the mold, the wick for the next candle is pulled into the mold (Figure IX.12). After many years of repetitious threading of the non-polyurethane molds, I wondered if the other molds could be treated similarly. I tried using long lengths of wick, attaching them across the top of the mold tubes using a bobby pin, and anchoring them where they come out of the tip with a sewing pin. The major problem with this method was that even with an extreme amount of pressure forcing the mold onto the damp sponge, the beeswax still had the tendency to leak out around the sponge-pin-wick-tube tip juncture. We finally resolved this problem by eliminating the sewing pin and holding the end of the wick tautly during the early stages of pouring.

Candle removal

The metal mold containing the candles should be allowed to completely cool overnight. Cooling can be hastened by placing the mold in a freezer.

To remove the candles from the mold, the mold should be turned over and the wicking running from the tip of one tube to the tip of the other tube should be cut in the center.

Sometimes by simply pressing the frozen candle further into the tube mold with your thumb, the candle will release. Also gently tapping the mold on a hard surface will often facilitate the release of the candles. If either of these methods fail, the candles can be removed from the mold

Figure IX.9. Simple coat hanger support pins position the wick during hot wax pouring, and are easy to remove once the wax has set to permit the removal of the candle from the mold.

by grasping the one-inch length of wick extending from the base of the candle using a pair of pliers and tugging on the wick while holding the tube of the mold under running hot water.

For the candlemaker who, in the process of attempting to remove the candle, has the wick break off, a cork screw can be screwed into the base of the candle, and the candle can then be pulled out while running hot water on the outside of the mold tube. Or reheat the mold and wax to remove the wax.

Support pins

Old-time candlemaking used to involve using single lengths of wick for each candle. A knot was tied at one end to prevent the wick from pulling through the tip of the mold tube and the other end was tied over some type of support bar such as a wooden dowel. This method often proved quite frustrating when trying to keep the wick on the support bar centered while pouring the candle and trying to untie the wax-coated knot at the tip after the candle was made.

• Coat Hanger Supports

We came up with a solution which eliminated these problems. We replaced the dowels with lengths of wire coat hanger which were held in position by placing them through holes drilled in the top of the metal mold (Figure IX.9). Using a candle mold with support bars-

1. Cut one continuous length of wick long enough to string all tubes of the mold. Allow approx. 12 inches per tube.
2. Thread one end of the wick through a doubled-over length of foundation wire.
3. Use this semi-stiff wire as a needle to thread the mold.
4. Start by threading through one of the small holes in the bottom of the mold (this will later be the tip of the candle).
5. Pull the wick through using the wire until only about 1/2 inch remains sticking out from the tip of the tube.
6. Insert a sewing pin through the end of this wick to prevent it from pulling out of the mold.
7. Take the wick-attached wire over the support bars (section of coat hanger), across the top of the mold, over the second support bar, and down through the second tube.

8. Continue with the wick-attached wire through the small hole of the adjacent tube, up that tube, over the support bar, across the top of the mold, down the next tube, until all tubes are strung with wick.

9. Pull the wick taut and secure the remaining free end of the wick with a sewing pin.

10. Align each wick down the center of each tube by sliding the wick on the support bar and bending the support bar if necessary.

11. To remove candles, pull out support bars, remove sewing pins, cut wick(s) connecting tube tips. Candles will be in attached pairs.

Polyurethane molds

Recently, candle molds made out of industrial quality polyurethane have become available (Figure IX.10). The advantages of the polyurethane molds over some of the plastic molds are that polyurethane molds have an extremely long life, leave no seams, do not require a cold water bath, give extremely sharp detail, allow for easy removal of candles and the multi-piece molds are held together with elastic bands.

To wick the tapered tube polyurethane molds, we use a piece of wire as described with the metal-tapered tube molds. With the figure poly molds, a Stole™ or Bodkin™ needle, available in sewing stores, does an excellent job. It helps to further sharpen the tips of these needles using a grindstone or a metal file. The needles can be forced through the poly molds using a pair of pliers.

The candles with bases approaching a diameter of two inches (5 cm) should be wicked with 60-ply wick while those of a lesser diameter should be wicked with 2/0 wick. Experimentation with different sized wick is sometimes necessary to achieve proper candle burning. The wick is suspended over the pour hole in the mold using a proper length bobby pin. If you are planning to make additional candles in these molds, leave the wick attached to the roll it came on (Figure IX.13). You can then wick the mold for the next candle by simply pulling the wick through while it is still attached to the candle being removed from the mold.

In melting the wax for the polyurethane molds, unlike the 180° to 185°F temperature recommended for the metal molds, the poly molds can be filled just as soon as the wax has melted. This reduces and sometimes eliminates the wax shrinkage as it cools and therefore reduces re-topping. If you get small bubbles on the surface of your candles, you might have to raise the temperature of the wax before you pour it. Candles made in some of the larger diameter poly molds often crack as they cool. This problem can be ameliorated by slow cooling.

When candles are molded in one-piece polyurethane tapered molds, they cannot be placed in the freezer because the polyure-thane contracts more than the beeswax, hence locking the candle in the mold. The tapered candles should be removed from the poly molds at room temperature and within 30 minutes of their pouring. The multi-piece figure poly molds can be placed in the freezer to hasten cooling, since the candles lift out easily when the mold parts are separated.

Figure IX.10. Polyurethane molds have an extremely long life, leave no seams, do not require a cold water bath, give extremely sharp detail, and are fun to use.

The bottoms of the figure candles can be further finished after the wick is trimmed by using a sharp knife or by rubbing them on the bottom of a heated frying pan, skillet or other flat-bottomed pot. As the melted wax accumulates, it can then be poured off and collected for future use.

Figure IX.11. Polyurethane molds are available in many interesting shapes, like these flowers floating in a dish of water.

Removing wax from surfaces

Melted beeswax adheres to surfaces, and it is one of the reasons why we suggest working on a tray and covering the area where you are working with a drop cloth. Melted beeswax will also adhere to candlestick holders if there is any dripping of the candle. If you spray your candle holder with

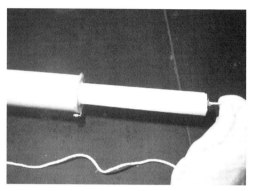

Figure IX.12. Tapered candles should be removed from the poly molds at room temperature and within 30 minutes of their pouring, since the wax does not shrink from the side of the mold.

silicone or cooking spray before burning the candle, any "wayward" wax will lift off quite easily. Since most of us don't remember to spray until after the damage has been done, placing the wax coated item in the freezer for a few hours makes it possible to chip off the wax.

Finishing candle bases

The excess wick at the bottom of the candle should be trimmed off for aesthetic purposes and so that the candle will stand upright in the candlestick holder. In the case of dipped or poured candles, their bases can be finished by either trimming them with a sharp knife, or by

inserting their bases in a hot plate heating device (Figure IX.14). This both flutes and smooths the bottom of the candles. The bases of the figure and pillar candles can be finished by using a sharp knife, or by rubbing them in a heated pan.

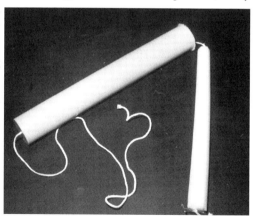

Figure IX.13. Thread poly molds once and pull the wick through the mold as you remove the candle.

Coloring wax

Whenever I do a beeswax workshop and discuss making colored candles, there is always an "old timer" there who insists on giving me a lecture that it is sacrilegious to modify the natural color of beeswax. We have found that many people like candles of colors other than the natural yellow. Beeswax can be colored using a number of different methods.

The ideal method to color beeswax for candlemaking is to use commercially made candle dyes that are available in many craft and hobby stores. To get these dyes to combine with beeswax, the wax must be heated to about 180°F (82°C). To get the candle color you desire, you have to experiment with dye amount vs. the wax's color. I have always wanted to make Wedgewood Blue beeswax candles, only to find that blue plus beeswax yellow produces a very ugly green color! We finally used bleached or filtered beeswax to make our Wedgewood Blue beeswax candles. We have also found that certain candle dyes can be used to mask darker colored beeswax.

Figure IX.14. Use a special candle base mold to shape the base of the candle. Use a solid hot plate and collect heated wax in a container.

For years, on other people's say-so, we recommended using Crayola™ brand crayons for coloring small batches of beeswax for making colored candles without ever really having tried it ourselves. Then one of our short course graduates started making large numbers of Crayola™ crayon-colored beeswax candles only to find that they didn't burn well. She found a reference in an obscure candlemaking pamphlet stating that the dyes in crayons tend to clog the wick causing the candles to gutter (drip) profusely and burn more rapidly. Upon learning this, we conducted an experiment using a number of different colored Crayola™ brand crayons. We used one crayon to color three standard-size tapers and found that they did burn appreciably faster than non-crayon-colored beeswax candles, the size of their flames were erratic and they guttered excessively.

Commercial food dyes available in the United States do not work because they do not combine with beeswax, due to their water base. We understand that there are some oil-based food dyes made in Scandinavia that do work well, but we have not been able to locate any.

We experimented with the powdered RIT™ cold water dyes, and found that they seemed to work but were concerned that they might produce toxic products when burned in a candle. We wrote to the RIT company, and they informed us that their dyes contained no toxic products. Their laboratory had already done work on making colored candles with their dyes, and they suggested trying between 1 to 2 teaspoons of RIT™ dye per pound of wax. Since their dyes are primarily water soluble, some dye particles will not dissolve in the wax. To keep the particles out of your candles, either filter the colored wax to remove the undissolved dye particles, or allow your wax to stand for a few minutes to allow the undissolved dye particles to settle to the bottom and then decant the colored wax off the top into your mold.

Satin finish

A very attractive satin finish can be put on candles. Select a watertight wide-mouth container deep enough to completely lower your candle into. Fill it almost full with water and heat it to the point where it will melt beeswax. Melt a thin layer of beeswax on its surface and completely dip your candle into the container under the beeswax layer and withdraw it. Experiment with the temperature of the water, the thickness of the wax on the surface, and how long the candle is submerged to achieve the desired effect.

A satin finish may also be obtained by rubbing the candle with a fine cloth.

Bloom

Often when beeswax candles are stored for a period of time in a cool place, a "dusty" appearing substance called bloom forms on their surface (See Figure I.8, page 21).

Rolled candles

Candles rolled from thin sheets of milled beeswax can be quite attractive (Figure IX.15). The rolled candles can be made from purchased sheets of unwired beeswax foundation, specially colored beeswax foundation, or thin sheets of beeswax you make yourself. You can make your own sheets of uniformly thick beeswax by using a shallow pan of the dimensions that you want your final sheet of wax to be. Add enough water to cover the bottom of the pan and heat adding enough beeswax until the desired thickness of wax on the surface is achieved. Once the wax has solidified, it can be removed by running a sharp knife around the perimeter of the pan to free the wax from the pan's edges. Working over a sink to catch the water, the pan can be carefully turned over to recover the sheet of wax.

Another method used to make sheets of wax is to dip a sheet of water-soaked plywood into hot wax. Make repeated dippings to obtain the thickness of wax you desire. Once cool, the wax may be peeled off the wood. A few craft wax suppliers will provide unembossed sheets of wax on a special order basis.

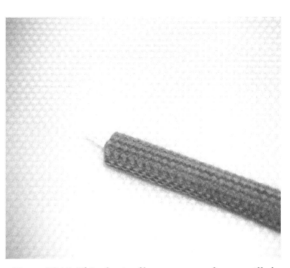

Figure IX.15. Thin sheets of beeswax or craft wax, milled with the hexagon shape, are easily rolled into candles.

Use these wax sheets for different effects. Generally, the candles are much more solid than candles made from embossed sheets.

If you are planning to make pure beeswax candles, be sure that your source of foundation is pure beeswax. Many embossed craft wax sheets are not made of beeswax: since the properties of paraffin are different, they are not marketed as pure beeswax.

To roll a candle from any of these sheets of wax, be sure that the wax and the place where you do the rolling are warm and the surface is clean. We generally make two candles from each sheet of wax, cutting it on a diagonal (See the drawings and photos on pages 106 to 108). Rectangular shapes are also made easily. Consult with the supplier of the craft wax to select the proper sized wick. Cut the wick for the finished candle and carefully begin to roll up the wax sheet incorporating the wick. The most difficult step in this process is the first turn, after that it becomes progressively easier as the candle grows in diameter. You might try flattening the candle as you roll, making a square candle.

Continued on page 109

Rolled candle suggestions

Craft wax sheets (which are milled on equipment used to make starter foundation wax for bees) are about 16 x 8 inches in the United States. Every country has its own "national" foundation size, so you will find considerable variation in craft wax measurements from country to country.

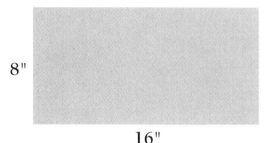

8"

16"

Rectangular shapes

Any number of length and width candles can be produced from the 8 x 16 inch sheet, and the direction of the wick placement, which determines which side you roll on, will determine the length of the candle.

For example, you may want to make the following candles from one sheet:

wick

To produce 3 cylindrical candles of different lengths and widths:

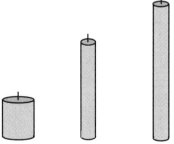

Diagonal shapes

By cutting the sheet on a diagonal, you can make two identical candles. The direction you roll the candle will determine the height. Two candles may be made on the same piece of wick.

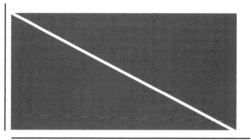

Wick position for a shorter candle.

Wick position for a taller candle.

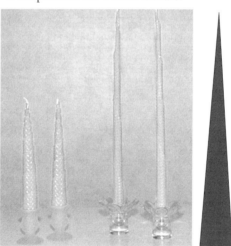

Figure IX.16. Short and tall candles, made from the same cut of wax, but different wick position.

By cutting the sheet into 2-inch strips, and then cutting each strip on the diagonal, you will produce eight 2-inch trees, which children enjoy rolling up!

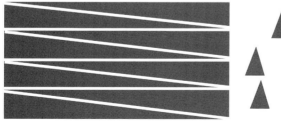

Put two sheets of wax end to end to create even larger candles.

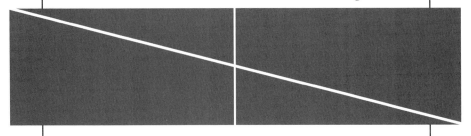

Other suggestions:

1. Use small cookie-cutter patterns to cut out figures to attach to the surface of a cylindrical candle.

2. Glue or tack on with wax any number of decorative materials: foil items, sparkling materials, small candy, sequins etc., for a decorative touch. Make sure the item will not flare when burned!

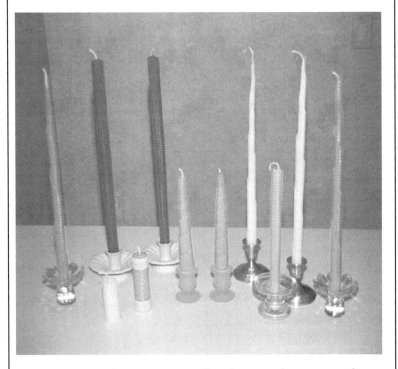

Figure IX.17. In an hour or two, you will produce many beeswax or craft wax candles for gifts, sale or personal enjoyment.

Hand-dipped candles

Dipped candles are made by repeatedly dipping a length of wick into melted beeswax (Figure IX.18). Select the size of the wick based on the planned diameter of the finished candle. Heat the beeswax just to its melting point. It takes 30 to 35 dips to produce a candle with a "standard" diameter base of about 7/8" (22 mm). The dipping container should be *at least* two inches (5 cm) deeper than the length of your candle. This reduces the number of times that you have to add wax to the container, gives room for the wax to rise when the candle is immersed, and prevents the dipped candle from picking up contaminants from the bottom of the container. Some type of double boiler arrangement gives maximum safety and uniformity of heating.

While small-scale dipped candle makers usually tie a weight on the end of their wicks, the weight is ultimately incorporated into the bottom of the candle which must then be cut off . We have found that by pulling the wick taut after each of the first few dips, that a weight is not needed. Also, to produce the "classic" dipped candle top, dip the candle a little above its previous top when the candle is about 75% finished. The dipped candle in the making should be quickly immersed in the wax and then withdrawn at a speed so that no wax is dripping off the bottom of the candle. By doing this and by allowing the candle to cool to room temperature after each dip, you will minimize the time it takes to make the candle. To speed the dipping process, some candlemakers dip their forming candle in cold water between each dip in the

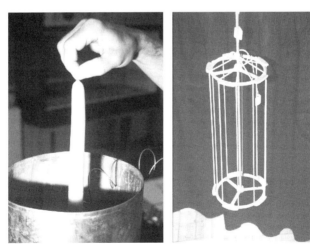

Figure IX.18. a (left). Dipping candles in a wax dipping tank. b (right).Protect your fingers— this device allows several candles may be dipped at the same time.

beeswax, carefully drying the candle off each time it is removed from the water. If the drying is not done carefully, a film of water can be left in the candle, often producing blisters on the candle surface upon the next dipping. Another potential problem in making dipped candles is when a drop of wax clings to the side of the candle. Remove any drops of wax by gently scraping it off with your fingernail or by rubbing it smooth with your finger. If you don't do this, the imperfection will grow with each dip. Small-scale dipped candle production is time consuming so we sometimes "cheat" a little and reshape a poured candle to look like a dipped candle and then dip it a few times for the final finishing.

Dipping should be done in a draft-free place. On one hot summer day, we decided to dip candles outdoors where there was a cool breeze. The candles we produced had some very unusual "sculptured" appearances!

To produce dipped candles on a larger scale, racks can be made, or sometimes found in hobby shops or from bee supply dealers. These suspend a number of wicks running from the top of the rack to the bottom of the rack. A number of racks can be used, alternately dipping them and allowing them to cool, thus greatly increasing the number of candles produced in a given time (Figure IX.18). The rack can be marked for the dipping level and again to get the classic dipped candle top, the rack should be lowered slightly below the mark for dipping after the candle is 75% finished. We use our wax processing tank for a small-scale dipping tank. Larger scale dipping tanks can be made from metal honey bottling tanks or from open top metal drums.

Figure IX.19. Candle dipping is an excellent demonstration for a craft show, especially if the older children take an interest in making and selling the candles.

Chapter X

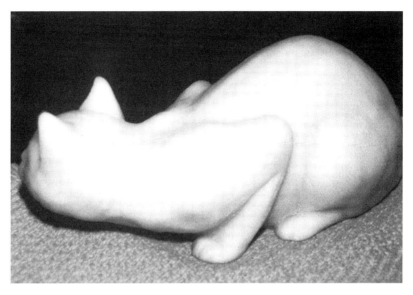

Figure X.1. After you have successfully made wax candles or beeswax art, try entering your work in a fair or craft competition. Unique molds, like the cat shown here and on the cover of the book, reflect control of a wide range of techniques.

Preparing Beeswax
For Show

Many honey shows include one or more categories for beeswax and beeswax products. Beeswax judging is somewhat subjective, with different judges using different criteria. Since the purpose of these shows is to make the public aware of the broad scope of the beekeeping industry and to help the beekeeper or craftsperson improve the quality of his or her products, you are strongly urged to enter your honey bee products in a show. Even though you may not win a prize, your entry will enhance the success of the show.

Through competition, you will learn what to expect from the judges and increase your potential for winning in future shows. Some general guidelines if you are seeking to win a prize are:

1. Be sure to read the rules carefully. I had to disqualify an otherwise first-place entry because the rules stated that its minimum weight had to be 5 pounds and the entry was too light.

2. Consult with beekeepers and craftspeople who entered wax in the same show in previous years.

3. Make sure your entry is submitted on time.

The Eastern Apicultural Society competition has 5 classes of beeswax entries including a wax block, three categories of candles and a novelty beeswax class (Figure X.2). For the categories containing pure beeswax, the following criteria are used:

Cleanliness	35 points
Uniformity of appearance	20 points
Color	15 points
Aroma	15 points
Absence of cracks & shrinking	15 points

Figure X.2. Many competitions have special classes for novelty wax, such as this molded wall hanging.

To produce show beeswax, start with clean beeswax. Start with 50% or more wax than you are going to need for your final product. Melt this wax in a stainless steel, Pyrex™, or enamel double boiler and filter it through a piece of sweat-suit cloth with its fiber side up (See figure II.4) The filtered wax should be collected in a spotlessly clean pan or dish with a smooth bottom. The inside should be sprayed with silicone or some other type of release agent. Remove the solidified block of beeswax from the container and scrape off any contaminants on its bottom using a sharp knife. Remember, beeswax is like a magnet for dust and dirt, so your hands should be clean when handling it, and it should not be allowed to come in contact with any surface that might have dust or dirt on it. When you are not working on your block of beeswax, it should be wrapped in plastic wrap to keep it clean. Repeat the above cleansing operations as many times as is necessary to get a perfectly clean piece of wax.

For good color, use only capping wax. Factors which can hurt the beeswax's color and which should be avoided are: 1. Allowing it to come in contact with metal, with the exception of stainless steel. We recommend melting beeswax in stainless steel, Pyrex™, or enamel containers; 2. Overheating the beeswax. This will darken it and destroy its odor. To avoid this, beeswax should be heated in a double boiler; and 3. Contaminants such as pollen, propolis and honey also discolor the wax.

To get a uniform crack-free block of beeswax for show, use a Pyrex™ dish to melt the wax in. Spray the inside of the dish with some type of anti-stick material like silicone or cooking spray. Melt in an oven, then turn the oven off and allow the wax to slowly cool overnight in the dish in the oven.

To maintain uniformity in your candles, we recommend that you make at least twice as many as you are going to need, and then carefully select those you are going to enter in the show by comparing lengths, bases, tips, length of wick, etc. All entries should be wrapped in plastic wrap as soon as they are finished and stored in a cool place in some type of rigid container so that they aren't accidentally marred before the show.

Ahead of the show, you should double check your entry and remove any bloom that may have formed on the beeswax during storage.

Figure X.3. A blue ribbon

Chapter XI

Sources of Supplies

B & K Books of Hay-on-Wye, Riverside, Newport Street, Hay-on-Wye, via Hereford, HR3 5BG, U.K. Supplier of obscure and out-of-print books on beeswax.

Berthold, Bob, Jr. 230 West Sandy Ridge Road, Doylestown, PA 18901. The author offers a complete line of metal and polyurethane molds, which he manufacturers. Also a supplier of general candlemaking equipment and lecturer on the subject.

Dadant and Sons, Inc., Hamilton, IL 62341. Offers general wax supplies, craft wax and stainless steel tanks for wax processing.

Hobby & Art Work, 10418 Timber Creek Drive, Kirtland, OH 44094. Phone 216-951-4997. Supplier of German-made poly molds.

Kelley, Walter T. Co. Clarkson, KY 42726. Basic candle supplies, tanks and other materials.

Mann Lake Supply, County Road 40 and First Street, Hackensack, MN 56452. Phone 800-233-6663 or 218-675-6688. Colored craft wax.

Maxant Industries, Inc., P. O. Box 454, Ayer, MA 01432. Phone 508-772-0576. Manufacturer of stainless steel melting/dipping equipment.

Mid-Con Inc., 8833 Quivira Road, Overland Park, KS. Phone 800-547-1392. General supplies for candle making. Advice given.

NORAC Chemical Co., 405 S. Motor Ave., Azusa, Calif. 91702. Hydrogen peroxide source.

Rady, J. Bavarian Wax Art. Box 2162, Anderson, IN 46018. Ukrainian Easter egg information and supplies.

Root, A. I. , 623 W. Liberty Street, Medina, OH 44256. Phone 800-BUY-ROOT. Supplier of beeswax and craft-wax foundation. The latter is a special colored foundation made of non-beeswax waxes which is used extensively in the rolled candle business.

Ukrainian Gift Shop, 2422 Central Ave. N. E., Minneapolis, MN. 55418.

Wicwas Press, P. O. Box 817, Cheshire, CT 06410. Phone 203-250-7575. Source of other books, slides and video programs on beeswax.

Chapter XII

Selected References

Alvarado, Barbara. 1983. Wax and comb in the life-cycle of the honey-bee. *Engineering* 110, University of Colorado, Colorado, USA

Anon. 1981. Beeswax on tree wounds. *Organic Gardening.* Rodale Press, Emmaus, PA.. USA. p. 10.

Berthold, R. Jr. 1987. Build your own beeswax processor. *Gleanings in Bee Culture.*115(12): 661-89.

_____ 1987. Building your own beeswax processor. *Gleanings in Bee Culture.* 115(12): 687-89.

_____ 1983. Beeswax and many of its uses. *Speedy Bee.* 12(10):4

_____ 1981. Beeswax. Part I. *Gleanings in Bee Culture.* 109(6):298-300.

_____ 1981. Beeswax. Part II. *Gleaning in Bee Culture.* 109(7):378-84.

Bisson, Charles S., G. Vansell & W. Dye. 1940. Investigations on the physical and chemical properties of beeswax. USDA Technical Bulletin 716. 24 pages.

Brown, R. H. 1981. *Beeswax.* Bee Books New and Old. England.

Casteel, D. B. 1975. *In* The Hive and the Honeybee. Edited by Dadant and Sons, Hamilton, IL, USA.

Coggshall, William L. & R. A. Morse. 1984. *Beeswax: Production, harvesting, processing and products.* Wicwas Press, Box 817, Cheshire, CT 06410 USA.

Cowan, T. W. 1908. Wax Craft-The history of bees-wax and its commercial value. Sampson Low, Martson & Co., Ltd. London, England.

Crane, Eva. 1983. *The Archaeology of Beekeeping.* Cornell University Press, Ithaca, NY.

_____ 1990. *Bees and Beekeeping, Science, Practice and World Resouces.* Cornell University Press, Ithaca, NY.

Dadant, Charles. 1983. Beeswax. Speaking at the New Jersey State Bee Winter Meeting.

Dadant & Sons. 1949. The honeycomb. *In* The Hive and the Honeybee. Edited by R. A. Grout. Dadant and Sons, Hamilton, IL, USA.

Driesche, D. V. 1983. Hand dipped beeswax candles. *Am. Bee J.* 123(3):

173-6.

Feinberg, Wilburt. 1983. Lost-wax casting: A practitioner's manual. Intermediate Technology Publication,. London, U.K.

Flottum, K. 1989. Brighter than bright. *Gleanings in Bee Culture.* 117(12): 693 & 695.

Furness, C. 1984. *How to make beeswax candles.* British Bee Publications, 46 Queen Street. Geddington, Northants, U.K.

Headings, M. E. 1983. Beeswax production and use. *Gleanings in Bee Culture* 111(12): 657.

Household and Personal Products Industry. 1982. Reprinted in *Am. Bee J.* 122(12): 822-823.

Hultgren, Kathy and R. 1985. Madame Tussaud's London Wax Museum. *Gleanings in Bee Culture.* 113(7): 365.

Homer, I. (1988). Odyssey. Ed. H. Bloom. Chelsea House.

International Trade Centre. UNCTAD/GATT. 1978. The world market for beeswax: a high-value product requiring little investment (Geneva: ITC, UNCTAD/GATT) 105 pp.

Krochmal, A. and Connie. 1989. Beeswax wood polish. *Am. Bee J.* 129(10): 655-656.

____ 1987. Beeswax furniture polishes. *Am. Bee J.* 127(3): 177.

Krochmal, A. 1987. A brief history of beeswax and some uses. *Am. Bee J.* 127(3): 176.

Krochmal, Connie. 1985. Hive cosmetics. *Gleanings in Bee Culture.* 113(10): 527-529.

Morse, Mary Lou and R. Morse. 1984. Painting with beeswax. *Gleanings in Bee Culture.* 112(10): 544.

Morse, R. 1988. Beeswax bloom. *Gleanings in Bee Culture.* 116(9): 514.

Root, H. H. 1937. Beeswax church candles. *Gleanings in Bee Culture.* 65(12): 724-725 & 767.

____ 1951. Beeswax: Its properties, testing, production, and applications. Chemical Publishing Co. Inc., Brooklyn, NY (*Apicultural Abstracts* 201/52).

____ 1951. Medical uses of beeswax. Beeswax: Its properties, testing, production, and applications. Chemical Publishing Co., Inc. Brooklyn, NY. p. 151.

____ 1951. Beeswax. *Cosmetics.*

Root, S. and R. Berthold, Jr. 1986. There is nothing baffling about beeswax. *Gleanings in Bee Culture.* 114(11): 573-75; 589-90; 596.

Rossi, Paulette. 1988. Beeswax used to soften skin. *Organic Gardening,* October.

Sammataro, Diana. 1989. Wax flowers. *Gleanings in Bee Culture.* 117(1): 20-21.

Snodgrass, R. E. 1975. *Anatomy of the honey bee*. Comstock Publishing Associates, Division of Cornell Univ. Press., Ithaca, NY. p. 144-47.

Sonnenschmidt, F. 1973. Art of Garde Manger. Culinary Institute of America, Boston, MA USA.

Stark, N. 1975. Beeswax for chapped lips. The formula book. Sheed and Ward, Kansas City, KS.

Sunflower, C. 1987. Beeswax ornaments. Eastern Apicultural Society Conference Workshop, Virginia Polytechnic Institute, Blacksburg, VA, USA.

Tulloch, A. P., 1980. Beeswax-composition and analysis. *Bee World*. 61(2): 47-62.

USDA Year Book of Agriculture. 1928. Beeswax dental impressions.

Van Driesche, Diana. 1983. Hand-dipped beeswax candles. *Am. Bee J.* 123(3): 173-176.

Wells, F. B. 1977. Hive product uses-beeswax. *Am. Bee J.* 117(1): 110, 114, 116, 150, 151, 160. 117(3): 150, 151, 160.

White, Elaine C. 1993. *Super Formulas, Arts & Crafts*. Valley Hills Press, Starkville, MS.

White, Jonathan W. Jr. 1966. Improving the color of beeswax. *Gleanings in Bee Culture* p. 742, 753, 758.

Wong, G. 1990. Beeswax and honey in cosmetics. *Gleanings in Bee Culture*. 118(10): 593-595.

Appendix A

Building a Solar Wax Extractor

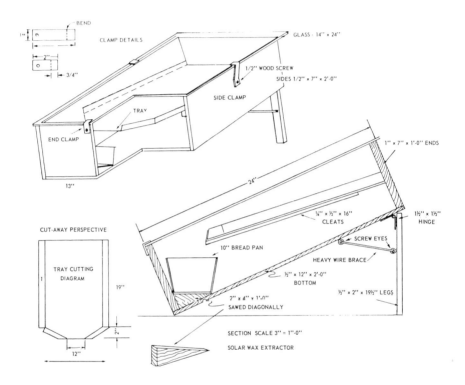

The plan above shows the simplified construction of a solar wax extractor, from the Ohio State University Cooperative Extension Service Bulletin 587, **Beekeeping Equipment**, Lawrence J. Connor, author. The plan on the page to the right was developed by Professor Anderson at Pennsylvania State University.

Notes:

1. Paint inside white
2. Paint outside black
3. Seal all cracks.
4. Place in a protected place on the south side of a building.
5. Remove wax and honey when most of the combs are melted. The honey should be discarded.

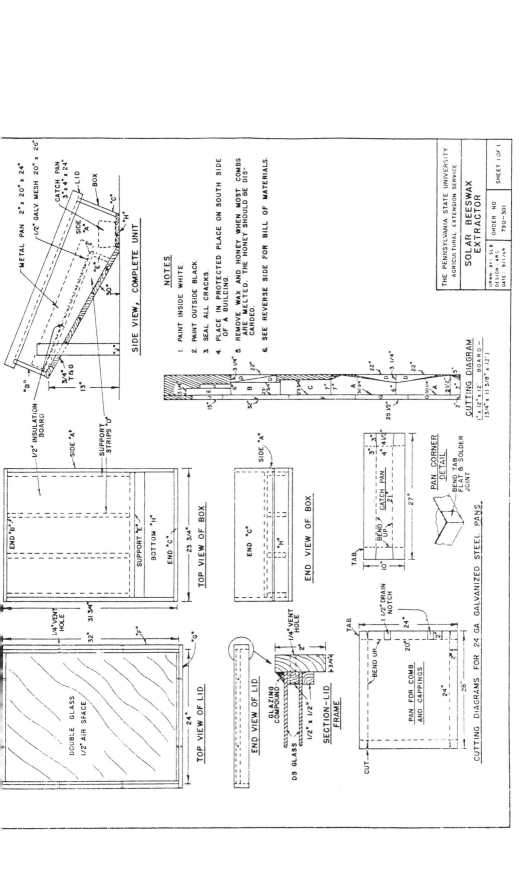

METAL PAN 2" x 20" x 24"

1/2" GALV. MESH 20" x 26"

CATCH PAN 3" x 4" x 24"

LID

BOX

SIDE "A"

"E"

5"

"H"

30°

"C"

"B"

3/4" T&G

13"

23 3/4"

SIDE VIEW, COMPLETE UNIT

NOTES

1. PAINT INSIDE WHITE.
2. PAINT OUTSIDE BLACK.
3. SEAL ALL CRACKS.
4. PLACE IN PROTECTED PLACE ON SOUTH SIDE OF A BUILDING.
5. REMOVE WAX AND HONEY WHEN MOST COMBS ARE MELTED. THE HONEY SHOULD BE DISCARDED.
6. SEE REVERSE SIDE FOR BILL OF MATERIALS.

CUTTING DIAGRAM

1" x 12" x 12' BOARD —
(3/4" x 11 5/8" x 12')

1/2" INSULATION BOARD

SIDE "A"

SUPPORT STRIPS "D"

END "B"

SUPPORT "E"

BOTTOM "H"

END "C"

TOP VIEW OF BOX

23 3/4"

31 3/4"

SIDE "A"

END "C"

"H"

END VIEW OF BOX

3" 3"

4" 4 1/2"

CATCH PAN

BEND UP

TAB

10"

27"

21"

PAN CORNER DETAIL

BEND TAB
FLAT & SOLDER
JOINT

1/4" VENT HOLE

32"

"F"

"G"

24"

DOUBLE GLASS
1/2" AIR SPACE

TOP VIEW OF LID

1/4" VENT HOLE

2"

GLAZING COMPOUND

1/2" x 1/2"

DS GLASS

END VIEW OF LID

SECTION-LID FRAME

3/4"

1/2" DRAIN NOTCH

24"

TAB

BEND UP

PAN FOR COMB AND CAPPINGS

20"

24"

28"

CUT

CUTTING DIAGRAMS FOR 24 GA. GALVANIZED STEEL PANS.

THE PENNSYLVANIA STATE UNIVERSITY
AGRICULTURAL EXTENSION SERVICE

SOLAR BEESWAX EXTRACTOR

DRWN BY: SLB
DESIGN A.P.S.
DATE 9/1/69

ORDER NO
790-301

SHEET 1 OF 1

Appendix B
Building A Wax Tank

The following section is included for the do-it-yourself type who is interested in saving money on a wax tank. This sort of tank mixes water and wax, which may result in a lower quality wax product. Readers interested in a high-quality wax tank should obtain a water-jacketed tank which keeps water separate from the wax. This also reduces the danger of boiling over, which the tank below is known to do.

If you do make such a tank, use it outside the house in a safe, wax-protected area.

—Editor

A wax processing tank is used to remove impurities and for dipping candles. We developed a beeswax processing tank which works best in handling beeswax that has already been partly refined to remove major contaminants (Figure II.7). It works well in heating the wax for making poured candles. It can also be used as a small-scale tank for making dipped candles.

Materials

1. Locate a container, preferably made of stainless steel. We obtained a stainless-steel container from a soft-drink distributor. The container was used to supply pressurized soft drink for beverage fountains. Larger wax melters can be made by using various sized stainless-steel honey bottling tanks and using higher wattage heaters.

2. For our heat source we initially used a ring (stirrup) immersion heater purchased from a farm supply store. We used the ring heater in conjunction with an electrical control regulator. Although we preferred the stirrup heater because it rested on the bottom of the tank, we made a functional melting tank by substituting a 1500 watt immersion heater which included a temperature control unit. The unit was tapped into the side of the stainless tank as close to the bottom of the tank as possible.

3. A nylon honey gate, available from most bee supply dealers

Assembling the melting tank

A hacksaw with a sharp blade is used to cut the top off the stainless-steel soda tank. A metal file is used to smooth the exposed edge.

Two holes were cut in the side of the tank, one as close to the bottom of the tank as possible to receive the immersion heater and the second about an inch above the top of the first hole for the honey gate. This was done by an electrical contractor who used a hydraulic tool that is used to cut holes in electrical boxes. A plumber's tank cutter may also be used.

The immersion heater and the gate are attached to the tank using rubber washers, gasket cement and proper-sized nuts to produce a leak-proof joint. Before you heat your first batch of wax, fill the tank with water and heat it up in a sink to make sure that it doesn't have any leaks.

A small petcock can also be joined to the tank as close to the bottom as possible. This can be attached by methods discussed above. This petcock can then be used to regulate the water level in the bottom of the tank.

Using the wax processor with water

Add water to the bottom of the tank to cover the immersion heater. Place relatively clean beeswax into the tank until it is about five inches from the top of the tank. This is an important precaution, since beeswax expands and foams when it is heated. If the tank is filled too close to the top, it will boil over.

I use water in the tank to prevent possible overheating of the wax. The use of water with a high level of impurities will cause the wax and water to bond (emulsify).

Turn the immersion heater up to the top setting and wait until the wax is completely melted. At this point, the power can be reduced until the wax continues to undergo a slow rolling boil. In order to produce beeswax that will make relatively dripless candles, the wax should be allowed to boil for at least 10 minutes. At this time, the temperature should be reduced to slightly below the boiling point, and at least five minutes allowed to elapse before drawing out the wax for candlemaking or for other uses. This allows any water vapor in the wax to escape rather than being incorporated into the candles. Candles with water vapor incorporated in their wax sputter when they burn.

Wax can then be cautiously drawn out through the gate valve.

Some notes of CAUTION—Cover your work area, including the floor, with some type of water- and wax-proof plastic drop cloth. Hold your wax pot under the gate valve when you open it and stand off to the side to prevent any wax from splashing on you. These precautions are necessary because if the tank is filled with wax the stream of wax exiting the valve can spurt out several feet!

When you complete each wax working session, be sure to completely empty the tank. Pour the liquid wax and hot water into a 60-pound honey bucket, filtering it through a piece of old sweat-suit cloth. Allow the wax to harden and pop the block of wax out of the bucket over a sink and allow any water to drain out. **If you do not do this, the wax will harden in the tank over the water. The wax may bond to the side of the tank when it hardens and when you restart the heater the expansion of the water under the hardened wax could cause an explosion.**

Sometimes while the melting tank is in use, the wax solidifies in the valve. If this happens, hold the wax pot at the opening of the valve and standing off to one side, open the valve slightly and bore a small opening through the solidified wax using the blade of a knife.

Use as a dipping tank

This same processing tank can also be used as a small-scale candle dipping tank. Once the wax has been liquefied and boiled for at least 10 minutes to produce a relatively dripless candle, allow it to cool to about 150°F (65°C). The level in the tank can be regulated by adding more liquid wax to the tank to raise the level of the wax, or lowered by draining wax via the valve or water via the petcock.

Index

Marren and Robert Berthold Jr. at a display of their molds and candles they offer for sale.

About the Author

Robert Berthold Jr. is a professor of Biology at Delaware Valley College, Doylestown, Pennsylvania, where he teaches biology andbeekeeping, and coaches cross country and track. He earned his doctorate in entomology from Pennsylvania State University. He is a popular lecturer on bees and beekeeping, and a leader in the field of craft use of beeswax.

Photo credits

Berthold Jr, Robert and Delaware Valley College: Pages 21, 24, 37, 43, 86.

Bossom, Michael: Pages 71, 74, 75, 76 (both), 78 (both), 79 (both), 80, 81 (both).

Connor, Lawrence: Cover photos. Pages. 1, 22, 23, 29, 30, 32, 33, 34, 47, 49, 50 (both), 51 (both), 52 (all), 53, 54, 70, 83, 84, 89, 90, 91 (both), 93, 94, 95 (both), 96, 97 (both), 98, 101 (both), 102 (both), 103 (both), 107, 107, 108, 109 (both), 111, 112, 113, 126. Most of these photos are available for sale, along with additional views, in full color, as the slide set # 38—*Beeswax Crafting Slides*. For informaton contact BES & Wicwas Press, P. O. Box 817, Cheshire, CT 06410.

Duffin, Elizabeth and Michael: p. 55, 56 (both), 57 (all), 58 (all), 59 (all), 60 (all), 61 (all), 62, 63 (all), 64 (all), 65 (both), 66 (both). These photos are available for sale, along with additional views, in full color, as the slide set #29—*Making Beeswax Flowers*. For informaton contact BES & Wicwas Press, P. O. Box 817, Cheshire, CT 06410.

Eastern Apicultural Society *Journal:* p. 44.

Maxant Industries: p. 31.

Peters, John: 110.

Williamson, Ray: p 15, 16 (both), 17 (both), 18, 19, 25.

Cover figure

The beeswax cat used on the cover and page 111 was made by Rick Freeman of Auburn, Pennsylvania. He made a mold from an existing figure, and cast the wax with that mold. The eyes were placed into the mold before casting. The piece was a blue-ribbon winner at the Eastern Apicultural Society of North America, Inc., Conference, July 1992, Guelph, Ontario, Canada.

About this book

This book was composed on a Macintosh computer using PageMaker 4.2a, importing text and image files from both Macintosh and MS-DOS formats. The text typeface is 10 pt Berkeley. The chapter headline font is University Roman. Most photos were converted to Kodak PhotoCD™ format and entered directly into the layout; the remainder were processed conventionally. Computer image setting and printing by Bookcrafters, Inc., of Michigan and Virginia.

Wicwas Press has published other books on bees and bee products. A free catalog is available by writing Wicwas Press, P. O. Box 817, Cheshire, CT 06410. Current titles include:

Coggshall and Morse (1984) **Beeswax: Production, Harvesting, Processing and Products.** 192 pages. William Coggshall studied beeswax all of his life, both academically and as part of his business. The book is the standard textbook on beeswax.

Hooper and Taylor (1988) **The Beekeeper's Garden.** 152 pages. This book shows what can happen when a beekeeper and a horticulturist write a book about bee flora which may grown around the home. There are many illustrations and photos, including a number in color. The book offers planting schemes and both species and variety names of plants which bees frequent.

Johansen and Mayer (1990) **Pollinator Protection: A Bee & Pesticide Handbook.** 212 pages. This is the most complete treatment of the subject of bee-pesticide interactions published to date. It includes the authors' and others' research findings on how to avoid pesticide kills while keeping bees.

Morse (1980) **Making Mead (Honey Wine)** 128 pages. Professor Roger Morse, Cornell University, has studied the production of mead for many years. This book provides clear and direct methods for the home brewer.